dux.se

TAILOR-MADE RECOVERY

Natural materials, craftsmanship and the **PASCAL**™ spring system makes our beds the best place for a continuous high quality sleep.

THE ORIGINAL SINCE 1926

DUX

MY LIFE DESIGN STORIES

Mondrian sofa and coffee tables, design Jean-Marie Massaud.
Stanford armchair, design Jean-Marie Massaud.

Monobrand: Goteborg, Casa in Corso, Ove Husargatan 12 | **Oslo**, Expo Nova Mobelgalleri AS, Drammensveien 134
Shop in shop: Copenhagen, My Project Copenhagen | Helsingborg, Indredningsgalleriet | Helsinki, Ambienti | Helsinki, Casuarina Herning, M3 Indretning | Reykjavik, Módern | Stavanger, Kielland | Stockholm, Ekerö Innemöblers
To find your nearest dealer www.poliform.it | Made in Italy

Poliform

Handcrafted in Småland, Sweden.

From our home to yours.

LAMINO easy chair. Design Yngve Ekström.

SWEDESE

QUALITY AS A TOP PRIORITY

Erik Jørgensen Møbelfabrik was founded in 1954 in Svendborg, Denmark, by saddlemaker and upholsterer Erik Jørgensen. Erik Jørgensen's collection consists of well-known classics from Hans J. Wegner and Poul M. Volther as well as new furniture produced in collaboration with upcoming designers.

We aim to produce furniture that lasts. Not only for use but also to beautify our surroundings, and open our eyes to new ways of seeing and making furniture. A passion for design and good craftsmanship is what characterizes Erik Jørgensen Møbelfabrik.

WWW.ERIK-JOERGENSEN.COM

ERIK
Jørgensen
THE MANUFACTURER

Existence is an exercise

LET THE NIGHT SET YOU FREE

As the day ends you step out of yourself and into something more sincere.
A perfect state of freedom. Carpe Diem Beds is the ultimate Swedish luxury bed.
Designed and handcrafted in Lysekil on the west coast of Sweden.

CARPEDIEMBEDS.COM | Model Sandö | Headboard Bornö | Fabric Luxury Light Grey

CARPE DIEM BEDS
SWEDISH LUXURY

© 2018 Residence Magazine

All rights reserved. No part of this publication may be reproduced, distributed or transmitted in any form or by any means, including photocopying or other electronic or mechanical methods, without the prior written permission of the editor, except in the case of brief quotations embodied in critical reviews and certain other noncommercial uses permitted by copyright law.

*If you wish to contact or follow us:
myresidence@aller.com
www.residencemagazine.se
@my_residence_bookazine
@residencemag*

*Residence Magazine
Box 27 160, 102 52 Stockholm*

*Repro: Bildrepro.se
Printing: Ljungbergs Tryckeri, Sverige*

Cover photography: Kristofer Johnsson

For your own copy of My Residence, order online at residencemagazine.se or email kundservice@aller.se

My Residence is distributed by Aller Media in Sweden and Arvinius + Orfeus Publishing internationally.

Please contact residence@aller.se or info@arvinius.se for questions.

EDITORIAL TEAM

EDITOR IN CHIEF & CREATIVE DIRECTOR
Hanna Nova Beatrice

ART DIRECTOR
Elisabet Magnusson

LAYOUT
Anna Hänström

EDITORIAL ASSISTANT
Rebecca Öhnfeldt

SUB EDITOR
Rosie Spencer

COORDINATOR
Anna Hänström

PUBLISHING DIRECTOR
Stina Abenius

ADVERTORIAL
Elite Media

Thank you to the editorial team at Residence Magazine and Aller Media.

SPECIAL THANKS

We are incredibly proud of our team of talented stylists, photographers and writers, without whom this third issue of My Residence would not have been possible.

PHOTOGRAPHY & STYLING
Photographers: Karin Björkquist, Bruno Ehrs, Lina Eidenberg Adamo, Lasse Fløde, Kristofer Johnsson, Mike Karlsson Lundgren, Erik Lefvander, Andy Liffner, Magnus Mårding, Pia Ulin, Michael Rygaard, Jasmin Storch
Stylists: Lotta Agaton, Annaleena Leino Karlsson, Louise Liljencrantz, Thomas Lingsell, Jakob Solgren, Hanna Wessman

TEXT
Hanna Nova Beatrice, Josephine Blix, Tom Cehlin Magnusson, Petter Eklund, Imke Janoschek, Hugo Macdonald, Michelle Meadows, Rebecca Öhnfeldt

TRANSLATION
Alexandra Svernlöv

CONTENTS

20 INTRODUCTION *Hanna Nova Beatrice*
Hanna Nova Beatrice is editor in chief of Swedish titles *Residence Magazine* and *My Residence*.
She has lived in her house, built in 1968, for five years; to her it's the best hideaway there is.

26 SLOW ARCHITECTURE *Andreas Martin-Löf*
Andreas Martin-Löf is the founder of the successful Swedish architecture firm
AML Arkitekter. He lives in Stockholm in one of the homes he designed with property
developer Oscar Properties.

34 FROM FASHION TO FRAGRANCE *Ann Ringstrand*
After 15 years at the helm of Swedish fashion label Hope, Ann Ringstrand
has started a new brand in her own name. Her family has a country house south of
Stockholm, where she goes to find peace of mind.

40 THE WHOLE PICTURE *Annaleena Leino Karlsson*
The interior stylist Annaleena Leino Karlsson recently opened her first studio space
on the island of Ekerö outside Stockholm.

46 A POETIC SITE *Mike and Conny Karlsson Lundgren*
Mike and Conny Karlsson Lundgren, photographer and artist respectively, spend as much
time as they can in their 19th-century house in Österlen, in the south of Sweden.

54 THE SIMPLE SUMMER LIFE *Gabriella Gustafson*
Gabriella Gustafson, one of the founders of architecture and design studio TAF,
designed her family's summerhouse on the Swedish island of Gotland.

60 BRANDED SPACES *Hugo Macdonald*
Hugo Macdonald, design writer and consultant, on how important
a space is to communicate a brand.

64 A PLACE THAT TALKS *Lotta Agaton*
Lotta Agaton is one of Sweden's most renowned interior stylists. She recently
moved to a new studio in Stockholm's Kungsholmsstrand.

72 A SPACE TO WORK *Hanna Wessman & Louise Liljencrantz*
Hanna Wessman and Louise Liljencrantz are two of Sweden's most influential interior designers.
They share an office and studio in central Stockholm.

76 BIGGER DREAMS *Måns Zelmerlöw*
The Swedish singer Måns Zelmerlöw has updated his Stockholm apartment
in collaboration with interior designer Hanna Wessman.

82 A CREATIVE COSMOS *Hertha & Gösta Hillfon*
Artists Hertha and Gösta Hillfon's home and studio affected everyone who visited.
Hertha Hillfon passed away in 2013: but we managed to capture the place and its spirit before
the house was sold and the objects scattered.

88 BUNKER ONE ZERO FOUR *Bruno Ehrs/Skälsö Arkitekter*
For more than three years photographer Bruno Ehrs documented
the transformation of a military bunker into a piece of iconic architecture.
Skälsö Arkitekter is the firm behind the transformation.

98 AN ACTRESS WITH A SENSE OF STYLE *Michelle Meadows*
Auction-obsessed actor and editor Michelle Meadows surrounds herself with one-of-a-kind
accessories and unique furniture.

104 QUALITY OF LIFE *Magnus Wittbjer & Micha van Dinther*
Micha van Dinther and Magnus Wittbjer run the online shop TypeO from their old
stone house in Hunnestad, south of Sweden.

110 A COLOURFUL PERSONA *Linn Eklund*
Linn Eklund belongs to the fourth generation of the family that runs flooring and textiles
company Bolon, which has coloured her aesthetics in fashion, textiles and interiors.

116 BASED ON A FEELING *Hugo Macdonald*
Hugo Macdonald on the unique appeal of Scandinavian interiors.

118 DESIGNS OF THE YEAR
A selection of the winners of *Residence Stora Formpris*, an annual award celebrating a year
in Swedish design, captured by Lotta Agaton and Erik Lefvander.

124 ONLY THE NECESSITIES *Joanna & Daniel Hummel*
Joanna and Daniel Hummel spend their holidays at the Bungenäs peninsula, part of the island
of Gotland. Here they have built their maintenance-free dream house.

130 TRIBE FRAMA *Niels Strøyer Christophersen*
Niels Strøyer Christophersen, founder of Frama, talks about the importance of spaces, good
collaborations. And the need for furniture brands to think different.

140 CREATING THE RIGHT FLOW *Sandra Adrian Asplund*
Swedish furniture brand Asplund is run by Sandra Adrian Asplund and brothers
Thomas and Michael Asplund. Sandra and Thomas's home, located on the Stockholm island
of Lidingö, is a personal extension of their brand.

146 VILLA ÅKERLUND *Ruxandra Halleröd & Lotta Agaton*
The majestic property Villa Åkerlund, outside Stockholm, has been turned into
residential apartments. The floor plan was created by architectural firm Christian Halleröd
Design and the interior design was by Lotta Agaton.

Hanna Nova Beatrice is editor in chief of Residence Magazine and My Residence. She lives in a house designed by Slovenian architect Radovan Halper. It was built on a load-bearing structure and is shaped like a mushroom. If you jump in one corner of the house, it can be felt on the other side.

INTRODUCTION

SOME SPACES affect you more than others. Most of the time it's an instant feeling; you open a door to something new and you are drawn to what is inside. Spaces can be interesting, comforting, beautiful and frightening, and even if you're not particularly interested in furniture or interiors, you are affected by what surrounds you.

To me, this is the most intriguing part of my work; the homes I get to visit, and the spaces I experience. I've always been attracted to houses, and I've always been interested in how our living spaces affect us. When I look back at my upbringing I remember it through the spaces I have lived in, and how they made me feel.

A visit to an art project in London in my twenties still stays with me. It involved visiting a house by myself. I received a key, an address and a set time when I was supposed to show up. I didn't really know what to expect when I put the key in the door – whether there were actors inside or if it was only myself exploring the house. I remember friends telling me they came out of the house crying. And I must admit, I was scared too, walking around in the grim three-storey house, not knowing what to expect around the corner. I opened closed doors and sensed the drama that could have been carried out in the rooms behind them. But nothing affected me more than the understanding of how much you can transform a space. Narrowing the corridors, lowering the ceilings and using colours and smells – just as you can add beauty and serenity to a room, you can also add fear and discomfort.

I have never been any good at creating a perfectly balanced interior. I fall in love with objects and they don't always fit well together. I guess the results are rooms with things that make me feel happy and at home, rather than looking photogenic. I prefer objects that have a value beyond mere function, a feeling that is hard to achieve in a world filled with mass-produced objects. A good friend of mine, who works with interiors, starts many of her projects by emptying a room, and then adding one or two objects or items of furniture that she loves. And then, step by step, a balanced and beautiful interior is born. This has never really worked for me, but I understand her affection for objects.

Every issue of *My Residence* is, in a way, a summary of a year in Scandinavian interiors, and reflects the tendencies, influences and thoughts that have occupied us. And more than ever before, many discussions have focused on the enormous overflow of products around us, and how we crave calm interiors with fewer objects.

This is one of the reasons we chose to theme this issue around the importance of space – the spaces we live in, work in or use to communicate ourselves or our brand. How can we communicate our values in a spatial experience? What do our values feel or look like? Hugo Macdonald has written about his experiences working as a design editor at *Monocle* magazine and brand manager at Studioilse, two organisations with very different approaches to space. We visit some design studios we admire, and some homes we love. One home, in an enormous military bunker, resembles a sculpture more than a traditional house. "It was love at first glance, a feeling of both fear and delight," says photographer Bruno Ehrs, who spent years documenting the transformation of this unusual space. "What was built for war is now built for beauty."

Be it a bunker, a summer cottage or a city dwelling, I want to thank everyone who opened their homes and studios to us in this issue.

Hanna Nova Beatrice, editor in chief
@novabeatrice
@my_residence_bookazine

PORTRAIT: JASMIN STORCH PHOTOGRAPHY: ANDY LIFFNER STYLING: THOMAS LINGSELL

INTRODUCTION | MY RESIDENCE 21

Wolfgang Tillmans
TASCHEN
Disegno.
THE CULTURE OF DESIGN
Disegno.
Olafur Eliasson
Disegno.
Nathalie Du Pasquier

Some favourites in the house: calming Smooth White colour from Jotun, wooden chairs by Swedish designer Staffan Holm for Hem and screen by Dry Studios, made in Stockholm. To the left: The hallway is only ten square metres, and most of the space is taken up by the staircase to the second floor, where the kitchen, living room and most bedrooms are located. The storage is custom made and painted in Jotun Lady Minerals Smooth White. The mirror is from Apartment Stories, and the bag is from Palmgrens.

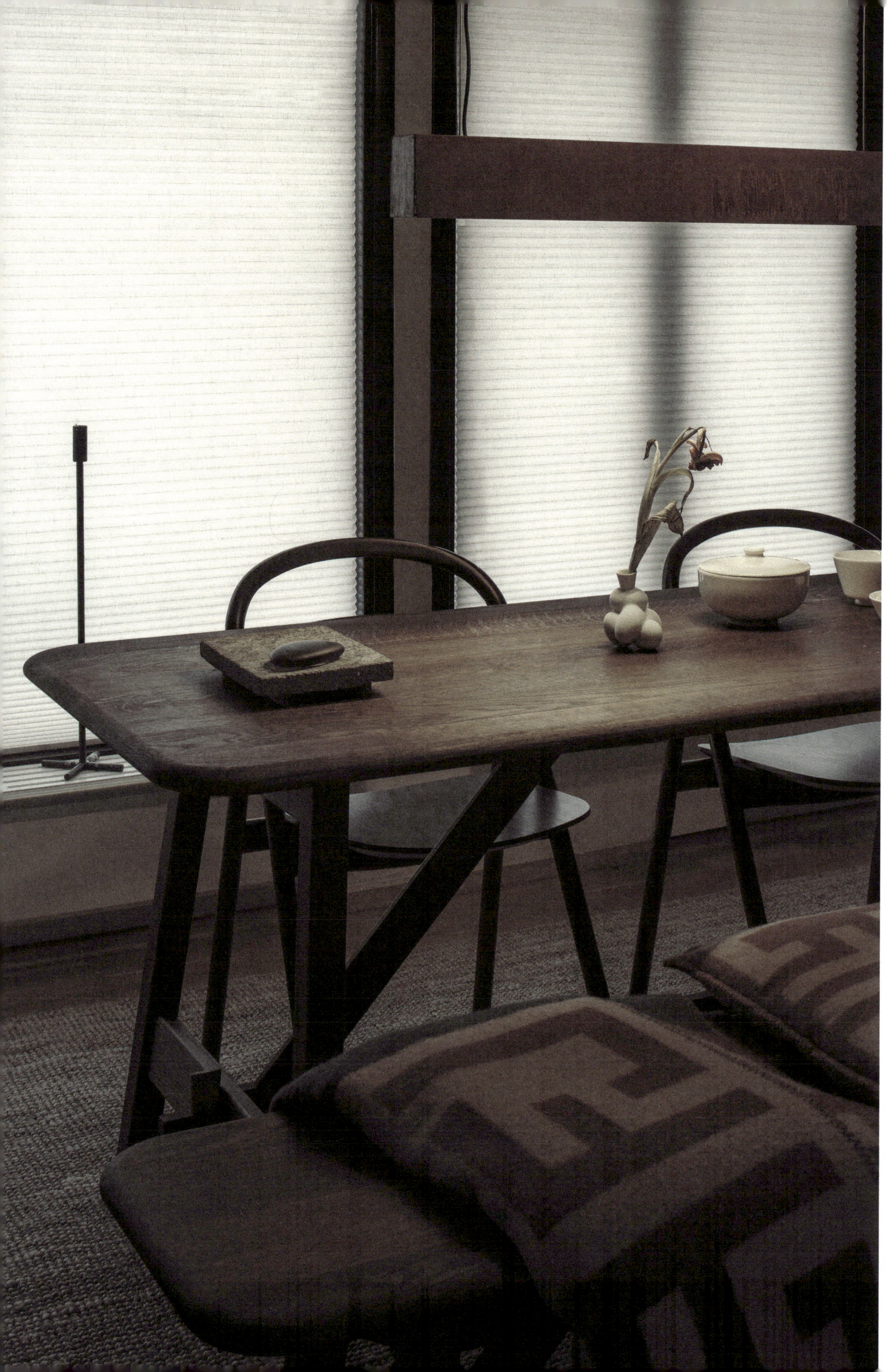

Above: Flooring by Bolon, with ceramics by K.H. Wurtz. Above right: Landala table, specially made in smoked oak, with Teema Tiimi kitchenware from Iittala and small Egg vase from Moooi. To the left: Landala table and bench, by Emma Olbers for Tre Sekel. The lamp is hand made by Studio Matti Carlson. The Duette Shades from Luxaflex create privacy while allowing the light to shine through.

Swedish architecture firm Andreas Martin-Löf Arkitekter is known for transforming culturally and historically valuable buildings in Stockholm into modern and exclusive homes. Andreas Martin-Löf also developed the Junior Living concept, creating small, quickly produced and inexpensive housing for young people. Martin-Löf currently lives in one of the homes he developed with Oscar Properties.

Slow architecture
ANDREAS MARTIN-LÖF

FOUNDED IN 2008, Swedish architecture firm Andreas Martin-Löf Arkitekter (AML) soon became known as a specialist in transforming culturally and historically valuable buildings in Stockholm into modern and exclusive homes – often with real estate developer Oscar Properties. Andreas Martin-Löf also developed the Junior Living concept, creating small, quickly produced and inexpensive housing for young people. The project is often cited as one of the few concrete examples of how the major housing shortage in Sweden's cities can be addressed. In 2014, Martin-Löf received *Residence Magazine's* Architect of the Year award for his renewal of Stockholm's residential world in two directions – the high-end market, but also the quality low-cost housing that is so essential in large cities. Today the architect lives in one of the Stockholm residences he developed with Oscar Properties.

Tell me about your home – what have you learnt from living in a place you designed yourself?

"My flat is located in the Pharmaceutical Institute in central Stockholm, and it's actually the fourth home I have designed and then moved into. I think I'm fairly unique among architects in testing my own works. I would encourage others to do it – it's very useful. In today's image-focused society one can easily forget that architecture is multi-dimensional and encompasses every one of the senses. In this project, I have over time become aware of unexpected and pleasant surprises – like the play of sunlight in the living room and the significance of the view, but also that sound behaves in a completely different way here with a ceiling height of 4.3m instead of the normal 2.6m."

Tell us about the building you live in and about your work with Oscar Properties here.

"The building I live in is part of the Vega block, located at Observatoriekullen in central Stockholm. In the 1860s the first Institute of Technology was founded here, and remained until around 1910. The first buildings were designed by Fredrik Wilhelm Scholander, and the expansion in the 1890s was led by Gustaf Dahl and Herman Holmgren. It is the seventh project that I have assisted Oscar Properties in implementing, and the first project where we have converted two designated historical landmark houses. The historical landmark designation constitutes the highest protection a building can attain in Sweden, and in this particular case there are more than 60 flats in different sizes. It has been a long process of around six years from the first sketch to the residents moving in, a period that has given us time for reflection and contributed to the success of the project. Few real estate developers and architects have that kind of patience; you might call it slow architecture."

What role has Oscar Properties played in contemporary Stockholm and the development of housing in Sweden?

"During the 13 years I have designed homes for them, they have always retained curiosity about what is possible within the framework of the projects, which I think is absolutely necessary for good housing. Together we have been able to create concepts that feel genuine and relevant because they take a serious approach to the building and its context. Oscar Properties has a special position in the Swedish market because the projects are bold, have creative originality, and are always a step ahead. In recent years more companies have followed in their footsteps, and the semi-premium segment has become overcrowded. The market is slowing down a bit now though, and I think those with experience and strong creative vision will benefit. I look forward to seeing the completion of the

PHOTOGRAPHY: ERIK LEFVANDER STYLING: LOTTA AGATON

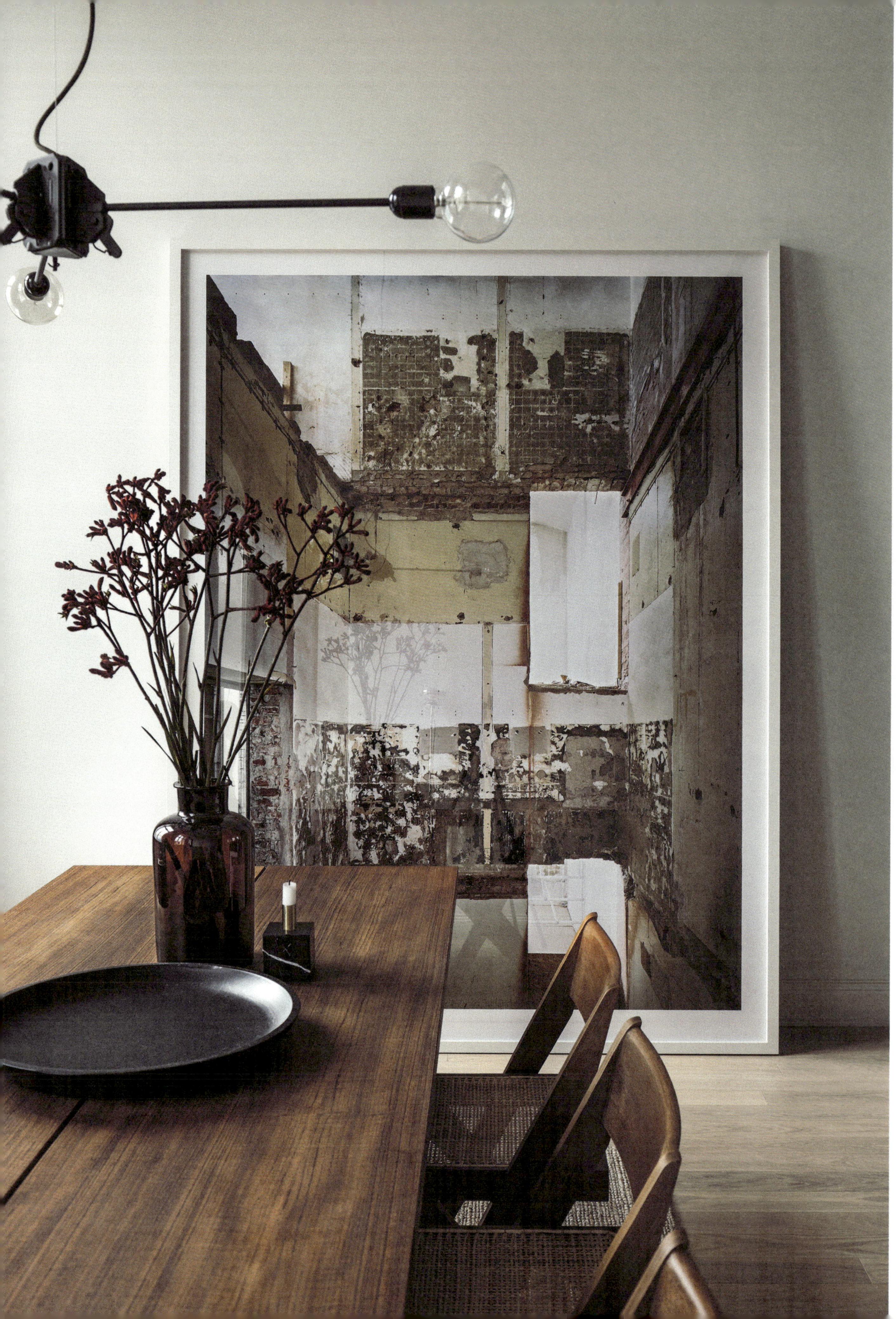

The round mirror in the hallway was designed by Martin-Löf. The bench in teak and the coat rack in black wrought iron were made by cabinet-makers K.F.K. In the background is a statue of David that weighs in at 170 kg, and was originally used for Martin-Löf's interior design of the Designbaren at the Stockholm Furniture and Light Fair 2016. To the left: The dining table in teak is designed by Martin-Löf and built by K.F.K. The library chairs in teak with woven rattan seats were designed by Pierre Jeannette and the photo is by Johan Fowelin, who photographed the building during the renovation.

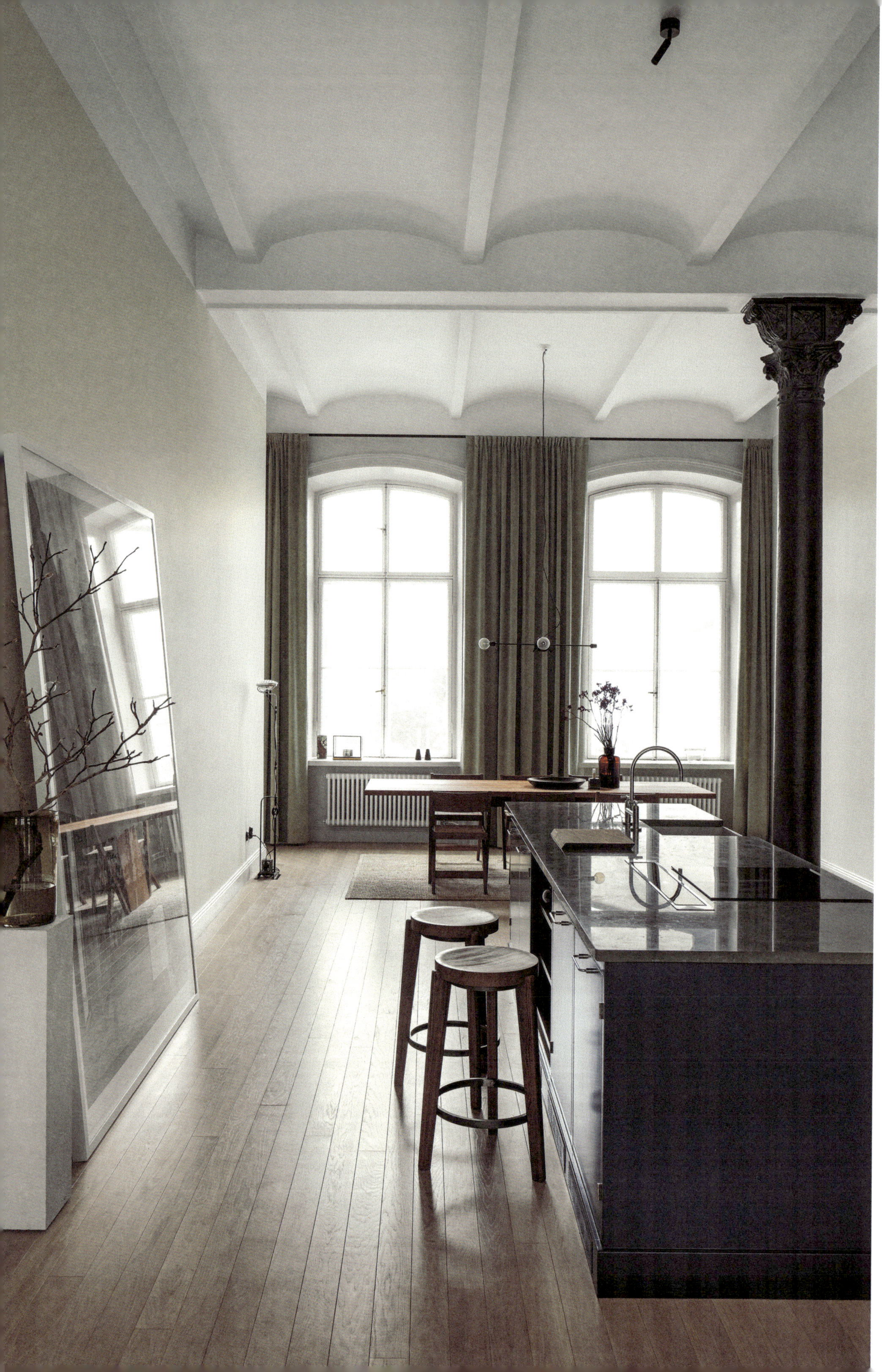

The original window has been renovated and the fittings and latches in steel and brass have been stripped clean of paint. The full-length drapes are from Astrid. To the left: The specially designed kitchen in laboratory green from the Swedish cabinet-makers Kvänum. Countertop in limestone from Borghamn. Stools in teak and iron by Pierre Jeanneret, and pedestal by Matti Carlson. The pillar in cast iron has a composite order with crossed torches symbolising enlightenment. It is unique to Martin-Löf's flat.

Northern Towers, designed by Dutch firm OMA, and Gasklockan, by Swiss architects Herzog & de Meuron. These are really exciting housing projects that will surely have a ripple effect in Stockholm."

Tell me about the interior at your place – what has been important from an interior design point of view?

"After a few years in my flat in the slightly darker Stråhattfabriken building, I dreamt about a brighter existence here. I kept my dearest possessions, and have had a lot of the interior custom designed and manufactured. The whole idea is quite simple – a bright base, with walls and carpentry painted a pale beige-grey shade, and a lightly pigmented oak parquet floor that contrasts with a darker green kitchen, reflecting the old laboratory decor. The limestone slab on the bench is of the exact same type used in the construction of the building.

The newly manufactured furniture is made of teak and hot-rolled and waxed sheet steel with details in brown leather. I reupholstered the sofa using custom-designed fabric from a small mill in Italy that was developed with Astrid textiles. A few chairs designed by Pierre Jeanneret reflect the renderings presented for the project and provide the flat with a sense of understated elegance. A massive photographic print created by Johan Fowelin during the construction period reveals the 120-year history of the building and six years of thought frozen in one moment."

What is most important to you in a home?

"I'm good at surrounding myself with a mix of old and new. Many of the old pieces are heirlooms and things that are special to me. By putting them in a new context they appear different, and I

The teak bookshelf was made by K.F.K. Martin-Löf inherited the Triplex lamp from his maternal grandfather, who had it in his lab in the building next door until the 1950s. The office chair is by Pierre Jeannette. To the right: Martin-Löf covered the sofa in specially made fabric by Astrid, woven at a small mill in Italy. The carpet in single-colour dyed wool is from India, specially ordered and finished with a hidden border. The armchairs and Kangaroo chairs in teak and rattan are by Pierre Jeanneret.

think it's easier then to see the beauty of such things. But my home is not a museum. It's more of an experimental workshop."

What do you bring from other homes?

"I think my upbringing in a very old house in the city led to me choosing similar places. There is something special about the generous ceilings and the meticulousness of the carpentry that attracts me to older architecture. The fact that I chose to move in here at the Pharmaceutical Institute may also be because my grandmother's father happened to be a professor of metallurgy with a large laboratory in the house next door. He also lived just a stone's throw away in Tegnérlunden – it's like historical land for my family here, which makes me feel connected to the place."

What would you like to see more of in Swedish architecture and interior design?

"I hope the trend for the kind of exaggerated experiments that have taken form in housing construction will recede and provide space for more thoughtful architecture, where solid craftsmanship gives the building its obvious value. Swedish housing is in a fairly weak place, and the current moment will probably not be remembered as a good time architecturally. On the interior design side, it would be fun to see more experimenting and less anguish. An interior that relates to both context and trends, rather than trends alone, lasts longer."

AML is celebrating ten years in business. How do you look back on this time?

"These have been some very intensive years. What I am probably most proud of is having managed to start up an architectural firm that, throughout all the projects that have been built, has managed to show that a different type of housing is possible."

By Hanna Nova Beatrice

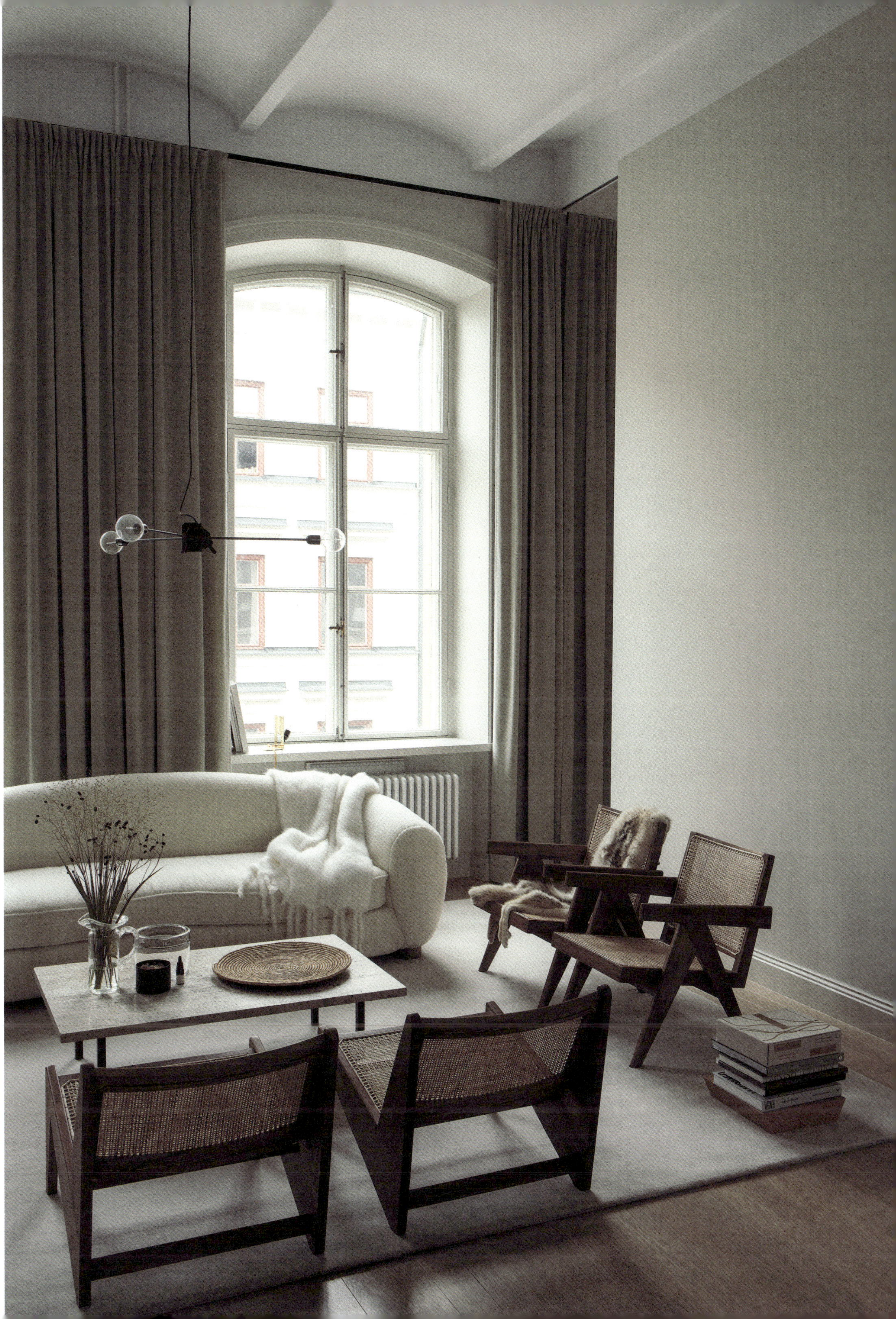

Ann and Jörgen Ringstrand. After 15 years as the driving force of the well-established Swedish fashion label Hope, Ann Ringstrand took a break, switching to a slower gear. This resulted in the creation of a new brand in her own name. At this stage, the collection consists of scents, jewellery, ceramics and relaxed studio wear. Jörgen, who, amongst other things is a photographer, is involved in the project.

From fashion to fragrance
ANN RINGSTRAND

IT WAS AFTER a major fashion show in Paris that Ann Ringstrand, founder and creative director of Swedish fashion brand Hope, stopped and tried to get her bearings. "It was a turning point for me," she says. "We had managed everything, the show had gone well, we had received good reviews. We had reached all our goals, but I noticed that I didn't feel anything."

As a regular yoga practitioner, Ringstrand had come into contact with mindfulness and the idea of being in the moment. "I started to realise that I very seldom was," she says. "For example, I did not really hear my children. I wasn't listening – instead I was planning the next meeting in my head. I wasn't really there." Ringstrand had by that time created hundreds of collections for Hope, which she founded at the beginning of 2000 with Stefan Söderberg. She met Söderberg while working at H&M. When he left Hope in 2014, Ringstrand began to reorganise the company, bringing in an external CEO and starting to prepare herself for life as an employee with less responsibility.

I meet Ringstrand at the country residence her family has rented since 2000 as somewhere to spend days off – the gardener's house at Elghammar Manor, a magnificent 1860s property in rose stucco, in the seductive Sörmland countryside around an hour's drive from Stockholm. You quickly sense Ringstrand's stylish hand in the house. The interior is filled with old wooden furniture, well-chosen textiles in brown and beige tones and black-and-white drawings on the whitewashed walls. It is cosy yet elegant, and you feel that the family has been settled here for a long time.

A year ago Ringstrand turned over the design responsibility at Hope to a new design manager, Frida Bard. "I really wanted to make time for a more active and present life with my family and I wanted to spend more time in New York," she says. "I felt like I wanted an opportunity to work there, and at a brunch in Greenwich Village NY, I said this to a woman I had gotten to know earlier – Maria Moyer, a ceramics artist. She shared a studio in New York with Lindsey Adelman, the famous lamp designer. I acquired a work table with them and started screen printing."

When Ringstrand had let go of everything at Hope except her seat on the board, she embarked on a training course in taste and smell in California. "Being present and using your senses more actively can be done in different ways," she says. "Identifying scents is one very effective way. I've always had a sensitive nose, and became quickly absorbed into this new world. I had a clear vision that I wanted to add fragrance to a room. But in the end I sat there for three days and found it extremely difficult. I caught myself thinking, but I must have known at least something before. Was I not,

PHOTOGRAPHY: ANDY LIFFNER STYLING: THOMAS LINGSELL

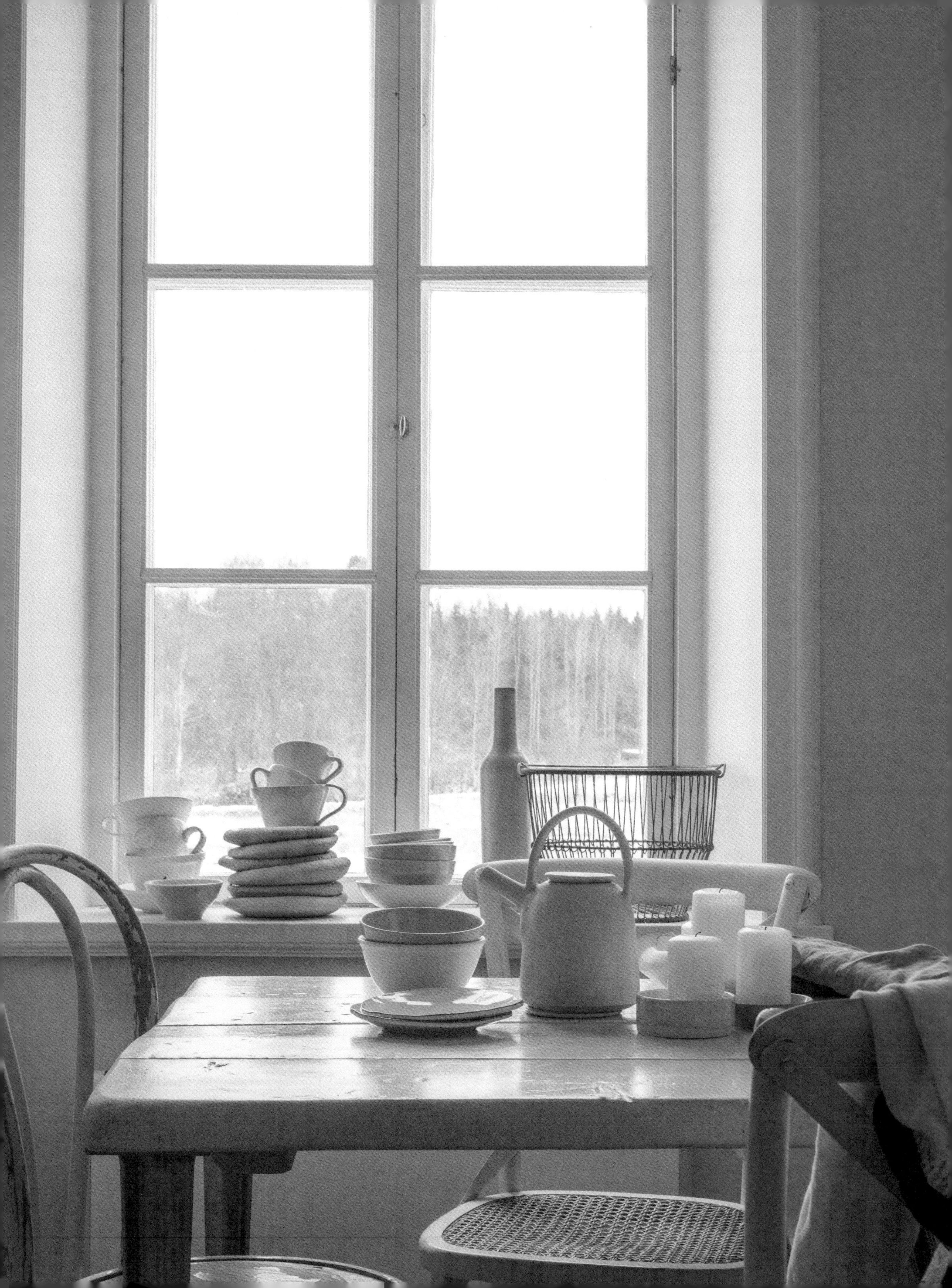

Ann and Jörgen Ringstrand have their country home by the Lockvattnet lake near the Elghammar estate in Sörmland, only an hour's drive south of central Stockholm. To the left: The all-white kitchen retains its 19th-century charm.

Ann Ringstrand's scented candles in ceramic ware are produced in Gustavsberg outside Stockholm, Sweden. To the right: The hallway has flows of light coming from two directions. From here you can look out to the gardens and the estate grounds.

for example, pretty good at fashion? I felt completely at a loss and like a true neophyte."

But after a few days things began to happen for Ringstrand. "I created three mood boards, just like when I was working with Hope," she says. "Three themes crystallised. The first one was about the relationship we have with ourselves – a kind of fundamental feeling of a heavy and rock-like calm. The second theme was about social relations, friends and family – very green and woodsy. The picture that grew out of this feeling was like a great big invitation. The last fragrance is the part of me I have shown the least. It's about togetherness. It is very close, has a lot of skin, and is sensual and warm – like the feeling you have after a long day in the sun. I'm approaching something new. Hope has always been all about function, a practical fashion brand. Here I work with something completely different."

By Imke Janoschek

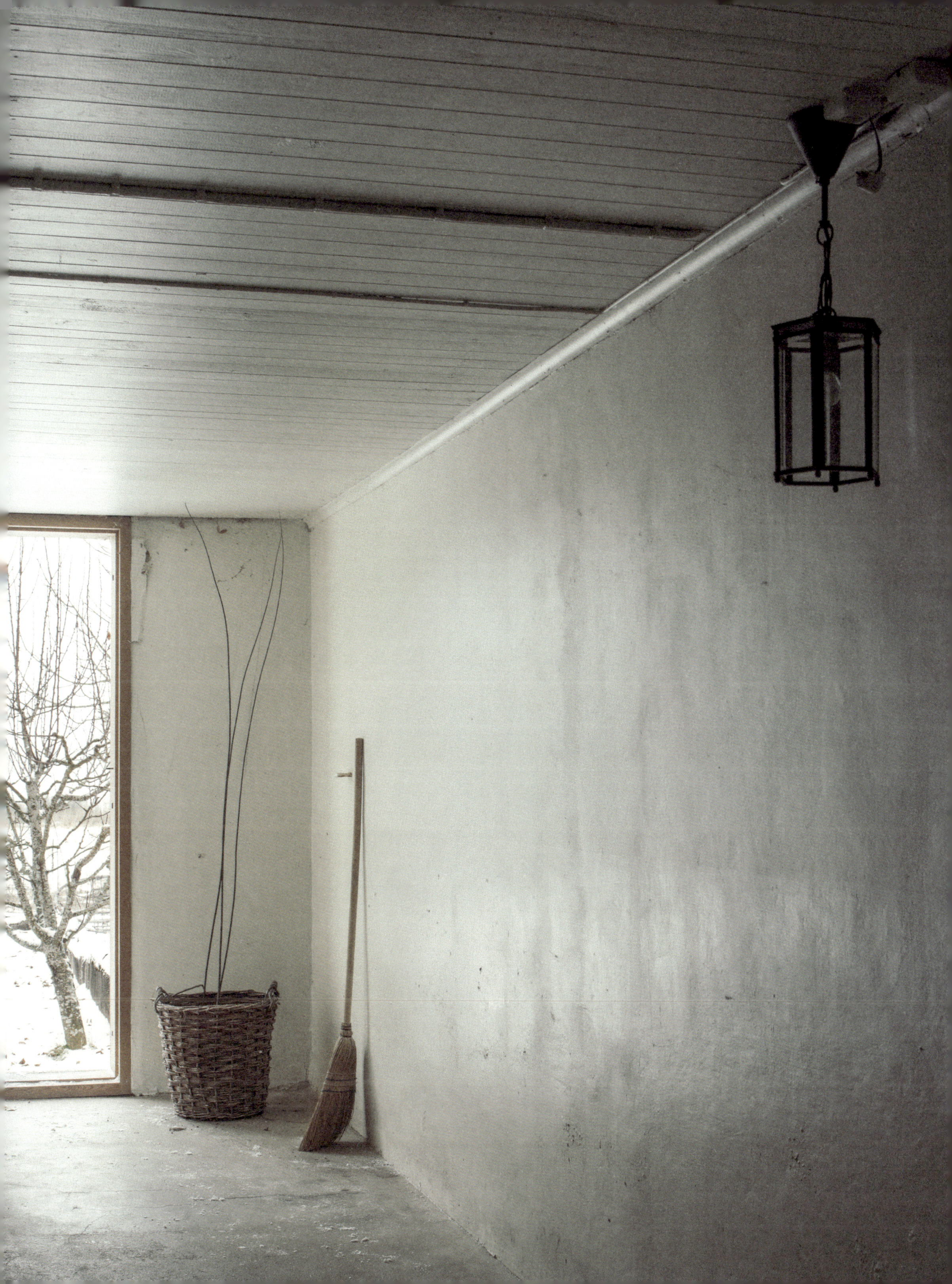

Annaleena Leino Karlsson is a Stockholm-based interior designer and stylist who has recently invested in her dream project, a studio near her newly built house on the island of Ekerö, outside Stockholm.

The whole picture
ANNALEENA LEINO KARLSSON

ANNALEENA LEINO KARLSSON started working as an interior design blogger more than ten years ago. Since then she has moved to Stockholm, started a career as an interior designer and stylist, and created her own collection of interior accessories. Now she has fully invested in her dream project, a studio near her newly built house on the island of Ekerö, outside Stockholm.

"I had long dreamed of a place where I could experiment with different expressions, show beautiful interiors, and highlight furniture and accessories in a sophisticated way," says Leino Karlsson. "This will be like a physical extension of the blog I once started, a calm oasis where people will come for inspiration. Everything I put here is available to buy or order, and the feeling should be like a complete home."

How do you use the studio?

"I moved here in the summer of 2017, and I'm still experimenting with what a studio can be. Today I use it as a showroom for various brands that I collaborate with, such as Hästens, Massproductions, Studio Matti Carlson, Wästberg, Kristiina, and my own studio designs of course. The studio is also available for hire for professional photography sessions, and I take photographs for social media for different companies. A showroom is a great way to communicate your aesthetics, and here it becomes clear how I work and that I always put the product centre stage."

Does it change?

"I change my showroom every week. New furniture and accessories influence the atmosphere of the room – a single piece of furniture can do so much. I really like clear shapes and contrasts. And I enjoy playing with different expressions and creating still life arrangements. Meeting with private customers is crucial, and it is important to be able to show the furniture we are talking about physically instead of only in a photo. To me, meeting people means a lot – to build a relationship with the customers with whom I collaborate and to understand their needs, as well as to inspire them with the furniture available in the studio."

How important is the image in your work?

"I create images for companies whose aim is to reach out with their products in different media. Often it's about putting the product or furniture into a new context, and getting both companies and prospective customers to see it in a new way. In my job as a stylist, the image is extremely important. But the whole picture is what's most important – the entire environment and how it makes us feel. In the future, I think that environmental considerations and long-term thinking will be increasingly important, and it will be important to make the right choice for interior design from the outset."

By Hanna Nova Beatrice

PHOTOGRAPHY: KRISTOFER JOHNSSON STYLING: ANNALEENA LEINO KARLSSON

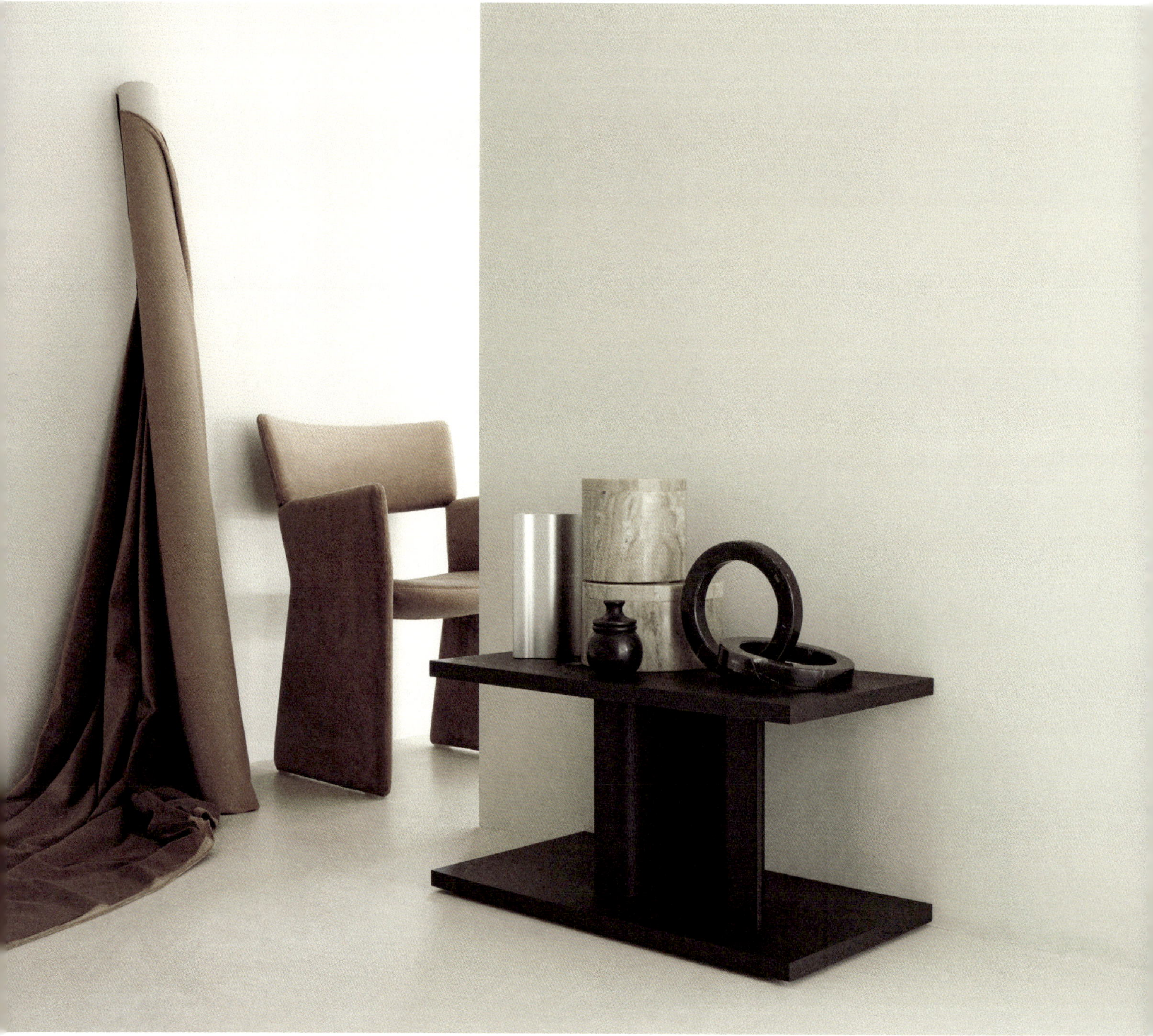

Leino Karlsson loves clear shapes and sharp contrasts. She redecorates her showroom every week and believes that one single piece of furniture can make a huge difference in a room. The black table and chair are from Massproductions, a company that Leino Karlsson collaborates with. The round black sculpture on the table is by Kristina Dam and the head sculpture is by Kristiina Haataja.

For now, the studio is being used mainly as a showroom for various brands with which Leino Karlsson collaborates. The round black clothes hanger is from her own Rail Collection. The pedestal is by Studio Matti Carlson. To the right: Sofa from Massproductions and a coffee table by Annaleena Studio. Black lamp from Wästberg.

"I CHANGE MY SHOWROOM EVERY WEEK. NEW FURNITURE AND ACCESSORIES INFLUENCE THE ATMOSPHERE OF THE ROOM – A SINGLE PIECE OF FURNITURE CAN DO SO MUCH."

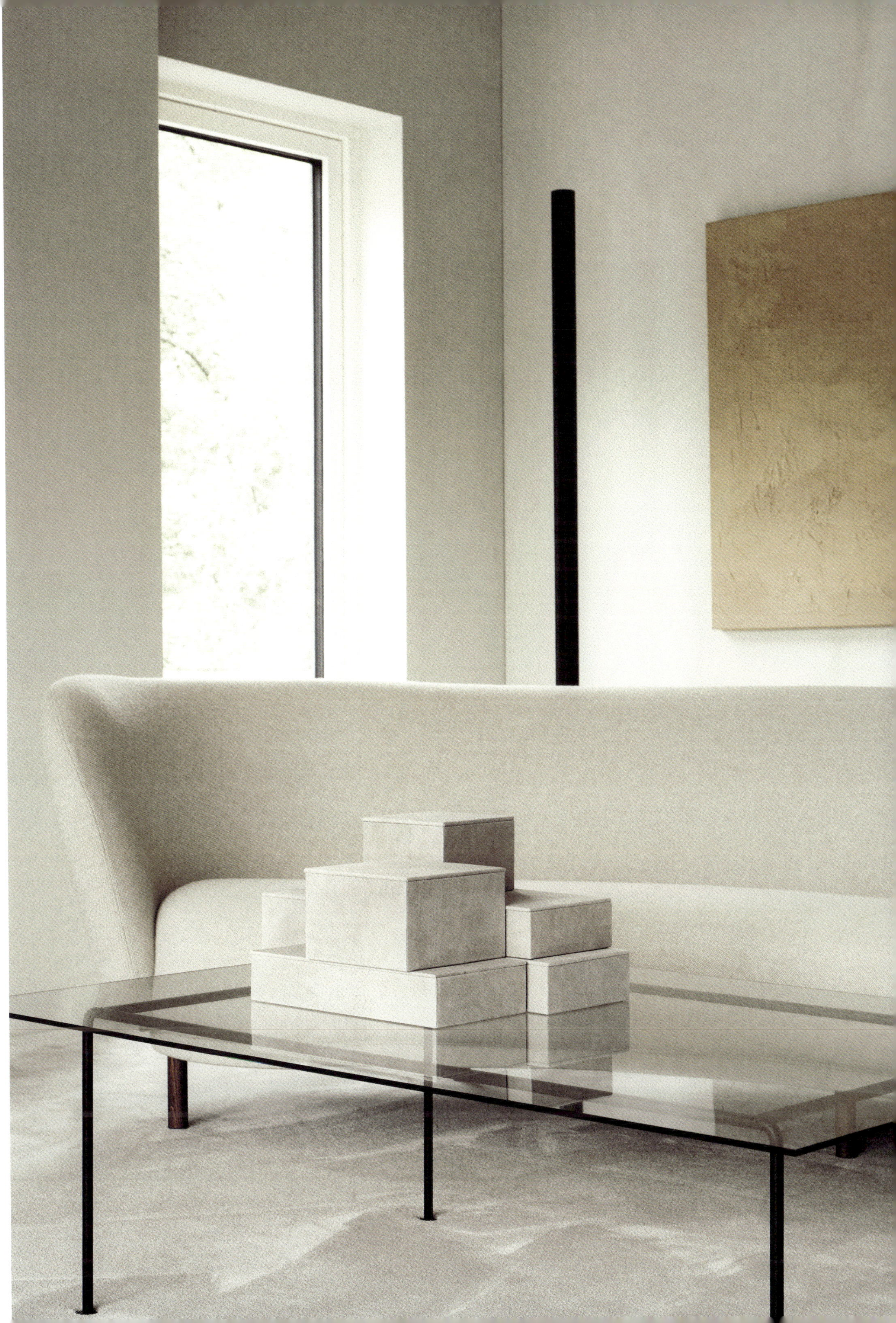

As often as they can, Mike and Conny Karlsson Lundgren, photographer and artist respectively, travel from their studio apartment in central Stockholm to their 19th-century house in breathtakingly beautiful Österlen in southern Sweden. Mike is currently working on several book projects, and Conny has an upcoming exhibition at Holstebro Kunstmuseum in Denmark in spring 2018.

A poetic site
MIKE & CONNY KARLSSON LUNDGREN

PARIS IN THE EARLY 1990s was the golden age of the great international supermodels. Chance had brought young Mike Karlsson Lundgren into the fashion photography scene, and in the next few years he would learn all there is to know about images in one of Europe's most fashionable cities. Along with photographer Mikael Jansson, he did a lot of notable work for prestigious fashion magazines such as *Vogue* and *Harper's Bazaar*, and he was given the opportunity to work at shows for Helmut Lang, Jean Paul Gaultier, John Galliano and Romeo Gigli. "The early years in Paris were an immensely creative and stimulating time," says Karlsson Lundgren. "The years I collaborated with photographer Mikael Jansson were incredibly educational, and during that time I developed my passion. The late 1990s and a few years later I spent in New York. There I had the opportunity to work with legends like Peter Lindbergh, Grace Coddington, Patrick Demarchelier, Joe McKenna and Fabien Baron. A great time."

After successfully working the international fashion scene for many years, Karlsson Lundgren and Louise Hall started the agency Hall&Lundgren in Stockholm, focusing on finding young talents. But today he is back where he started, in some ways. "I broadened my overall knowledge and experience with further training, and now I'm active in the area of photography for which I feel so strongly – poetic environments, still life, decoration and portraits," he says. "Staged photos with ambience inspire me."

For the past seven years Karlsson Lundgren has lived with artist Conny Karlsson Lundgren. They met in Berlin, but soon after they moved to New York, and that's where they married in 2012. The following year they settled in Stockholm, although Conny often travels for work. "I exhibit both in Sweden and internationally and travel a lot in connection with exhibitions and studio fellowships," he says. "I explore fragments of historical events that have shaped a community in different ways, and my work is often based on feminist and queer stories. It gives me the privilege of staying in places I probably would not have visited otherwise, like Tirana, Northampton and most recently one year in a small university town in southern Holland."

After spending a lot of time away from each other in different parts of the world, the couple's yearning for a summerhouse began to grow stronger. It felt more and more enticing to have a fixed point, and after a couple of lovely summer weeks on the eastern side of Skåne in southern Sweden, the search began. At the end of 2014 they found their house in southern Österlen. It's a classic Skåne summerhouse situated in the midst of open cultivated fields, with a beautiful garden guarded by two large trees – a chestnut and a maple. "The first time I visited the house was a rough November day when the fields were wrapped in a warm grey mist," says Mike. "I sent pictures to Conny, who was in Maastricht, and we both knew this had to be the house. If it could be so beautiful in a gloomy winter month, what could it not deliver in the summer?" At the turn of the year, the Skåne house was theirs. In Stockholm they exchanged their large apartment for a smaller studio flat in the centre of town. "The home in Stockholm we keep a little simpler

PHOTOGRAPHY: MIKE KARLSSON LUNDGREN

MIKE & CONNY KARLSSON LUNDGREN | MY RESIDENCE 47

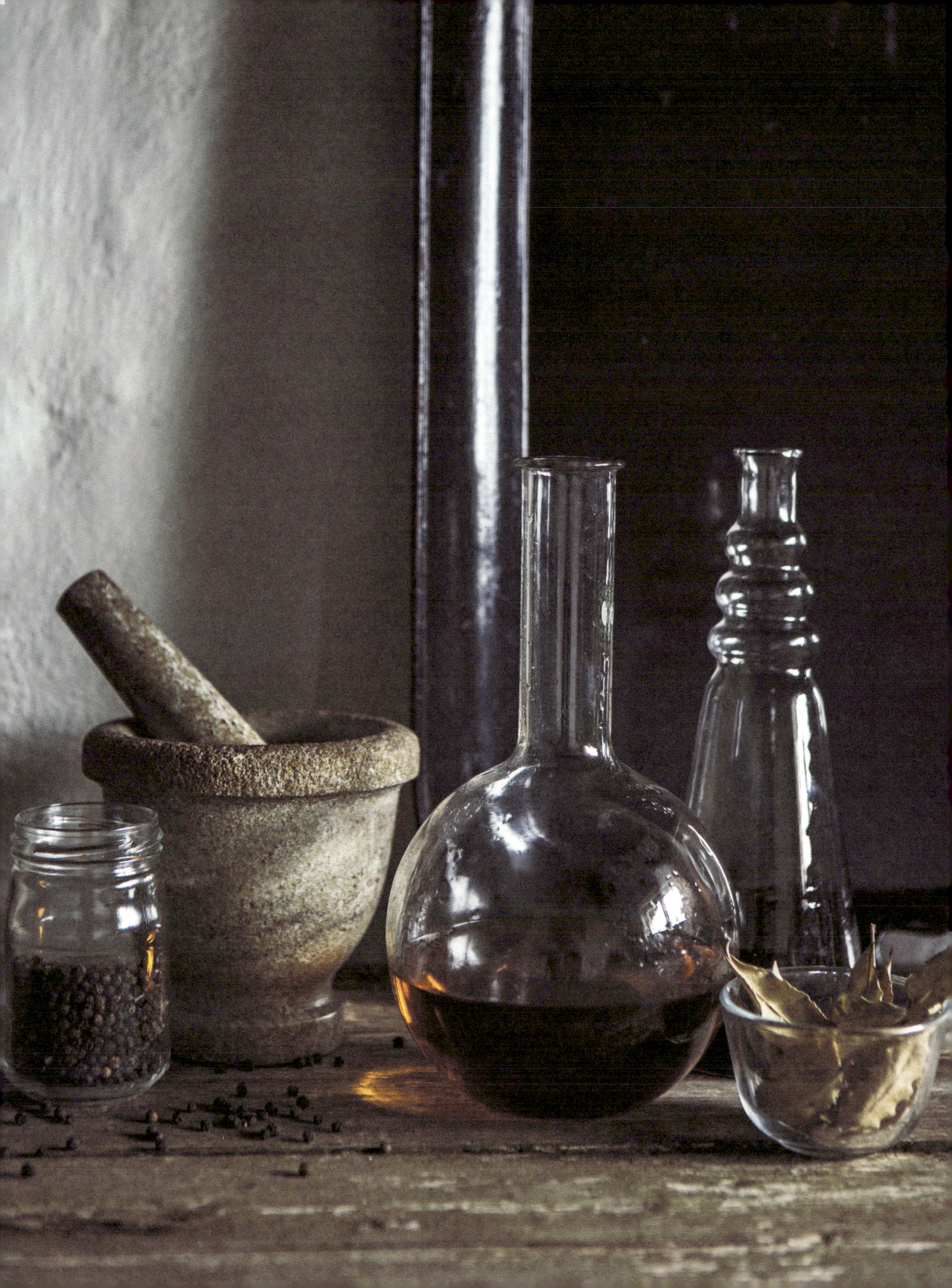

The beach where Mike and Conny take long walks throughout the year is called Mälarhusen. To the left: Every detail counts. Spices, oil and vinegar are all poured into beautiful vintage glass holders.

MIKE & CONNY KARLSSON LUNDGREN | MY RESIDENCE 50

Two-and-a-half-metre long and very heavy dining table, a solid oak plank on trestles, was transported with great effort from the couple's home in Stockholm. The view provides magical sunsets over fields and meadows. Above the dining table hangs a brass lamp they found at a flea market, which they later found out was designed by Hans-Agne Jakobsson. The door to the kitchen often stands open so that the person doing the cooking can partake in the conversation.

The house has white stucco walls and wooden ceilings painted white, except for the dining room where the couple decided to keep the black painted ceiling. On the handcrafted shelf there are ceramic creations by Lotta Jansson, who is a friend of Mike and Conny. To the right: The couple often use the decorative antique stove, known as a sättugn in Swedish, which is typical in the southern part of Skåne. Conny constructed the massive wooden counter top, which was originally part of an art exhibition. For now it's being used to store wood, and with two vintage pillows on top it makes a great viewing spot.

and more ascetic, but down here we go with the flow, whatever feels right," says Mike. "There are plenty of flea markets here and it is a fun way to add and blend in things from our past lives."

No major alterations on the house were necessary, with the exception of some surface renovation and projects that they could handle themselves. Mike has always dreamt of having a real garden, so when they took over the house the plot went through a transformation. "The basics were all in place with its nice structure and classic country cottage plants, but we added lots of roses, lavender, autumnal anemones, a herb garden and a vegetable garden," he says. "Now the front of the house is completely embedded in a cottage garden, while the back is left free, simple and wild with the fields close by."

Since the journey between Stockholm and Skåne is quite long, the idea was initially that the couple would spend summers and long weekends in the house. But it turns out that the house has a magical feeling in all seasons. "You can feel the proximity to the ocean in the air," says Mike. "Perhaps we appreciate it a little bit more when the summer is waning and it feels like the beach is ours alone. During certain periods we feel optimistically self-sufficient with our little vegetable garden, and our otherwise reticent little Eddie has become a rugged farm dog watching over the premises. Sometimes we play with the idea of staying here year round. At the same time we really enjoy the contrast between the city life and our existence here."

By Josephine Blix

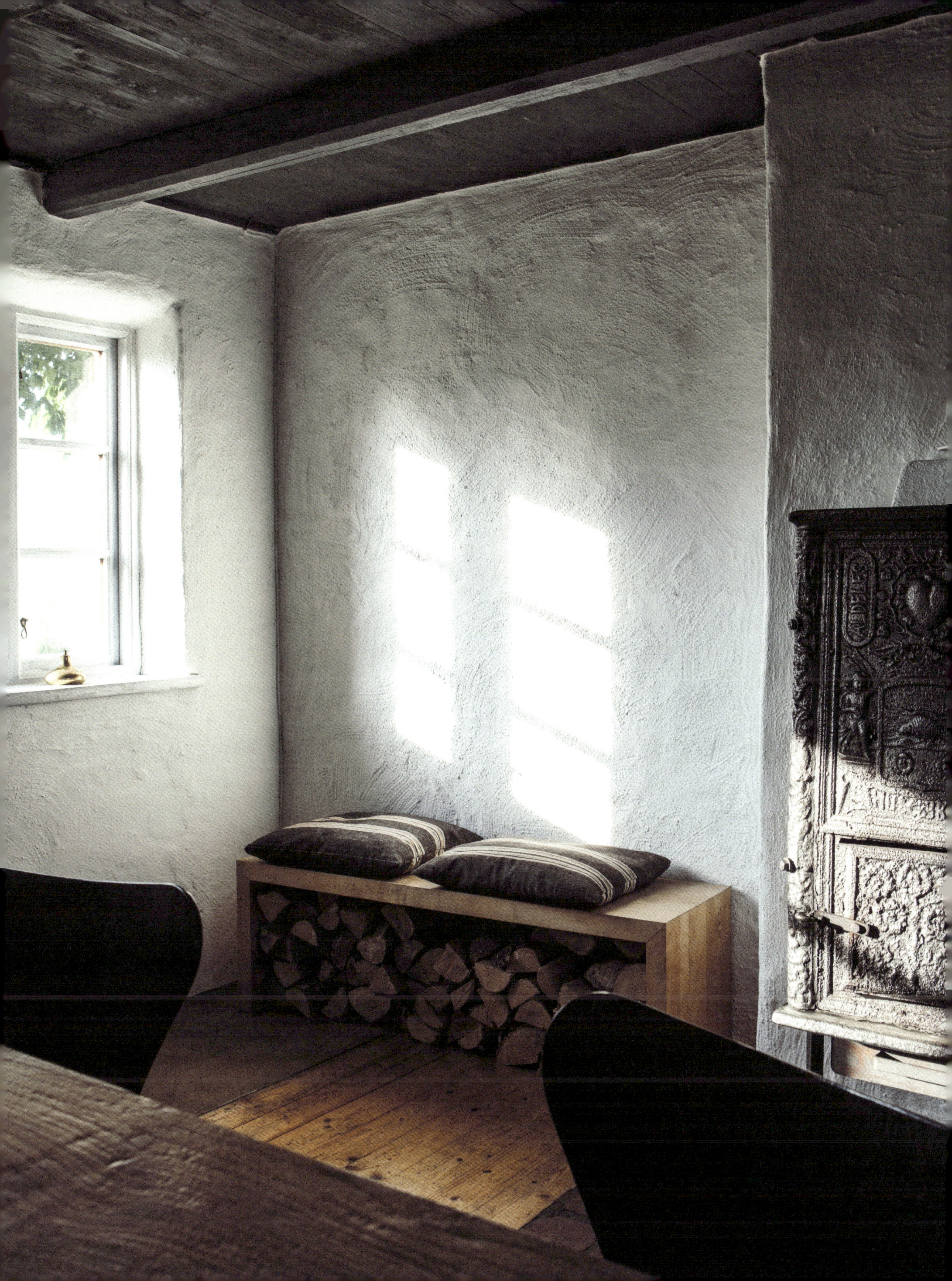

Gabriella Gustafson, one half of Swedish architecture and design duo TAF, designed a private summerhouse on the island of Gotland for her family. With an interior made of wood, it was created for simple living by the sea. The house's shell is made of processed sheet metal, to make it maintenance free.

The simple summer life
GABRIELLA GUSTAFSON

FIVE PEOPLE IN a circus wagon – that's how the Gustafson family spent three summers on their undeveloped land on the Swedish holiday island of Gotland. "Circus wagon is more of a nickname – it was really a construction shed on wheels that we bought, refurbished and transported there after we bought the plot," says Gabriella Gustafson, one half of renowned architecture and design duo TAF. Based in Stockholm, the studio was founded by Gustafson and her colleague Mattias Ståhlbom in 2002. This year the pair received the most prestigious design award that Sweden has to offer, the Bruno Mathsson Prize, for the refined simplicity of their design language, which combines humour and boldness.

TAF's signature is finding everyday materials that inspire a new product or environment. An ice cream bar was the inspiration for the interior of a Camper shop, while soda cans were the influence for one of the duo's lamp designs. Their best-known products are produced by companies such as Fogia, Muuto, Arita and NakNak. These include the Wood desk light for Danish firm Muuto, made entirely from wood, and recently the Bleck sofa for Swedish furniture manufacturer Gärsnäs. This year TAF is creating a new restaurant and café for the National Museum in Stockholm.

But despite several prestigious architecture and design projects, Gustafson had yet to design her own family home. "There is some pressure," she says. "You have a responsibility for it being right, both for yourself and also because people are watching."

After three summers in the 12-square-metre construction shed with no running water, it was time to break ground. There were a couple of fixed parameters that Gustafson set from the start. "We wanted to build a wooden house that was maintenance free," she says. "Neither of us wanted to stand there on holiday with brush in hand painting the facade. It was important that the house be robust, simple and durable. It should be possible to hammer a nail into the wall, and it shouldn't matter if someone spills water." The structure was made from KL-wood (cross-laminated timber) – solid wooden slabs that are cross-glued and provide a very stable building material. "It's sort of like you're building with Lego," says Gustafson.

The end result was a large cabin with three bedrooms, heated by a wood stove. Details such as sliding windows and doors bear a similarity to some of TAF's products. The house was erected in four months and the family used it straight away during the first summer. "The previous three years it felt almost like we stayed in a tent, with a lot of outdoor living," says Gustafson. "So the feeling of comfort is great now. As long as you're just a small family, you can have the simple summer life where you get water from the well and wash everything by hand. It's a liberating experience. Some things simply take time, such as washing or going for a bath in the lime quarry. But needs change when, for example, people come to visit, and there may be things that the children will want as they grow older. Eventually it will feel good to plug in a dishwasher."

By Imke Janoschek

PHOTOGRAPHY: ERIK LEFVANDER STYLING: ANNALEENA LEINO KARLSSON

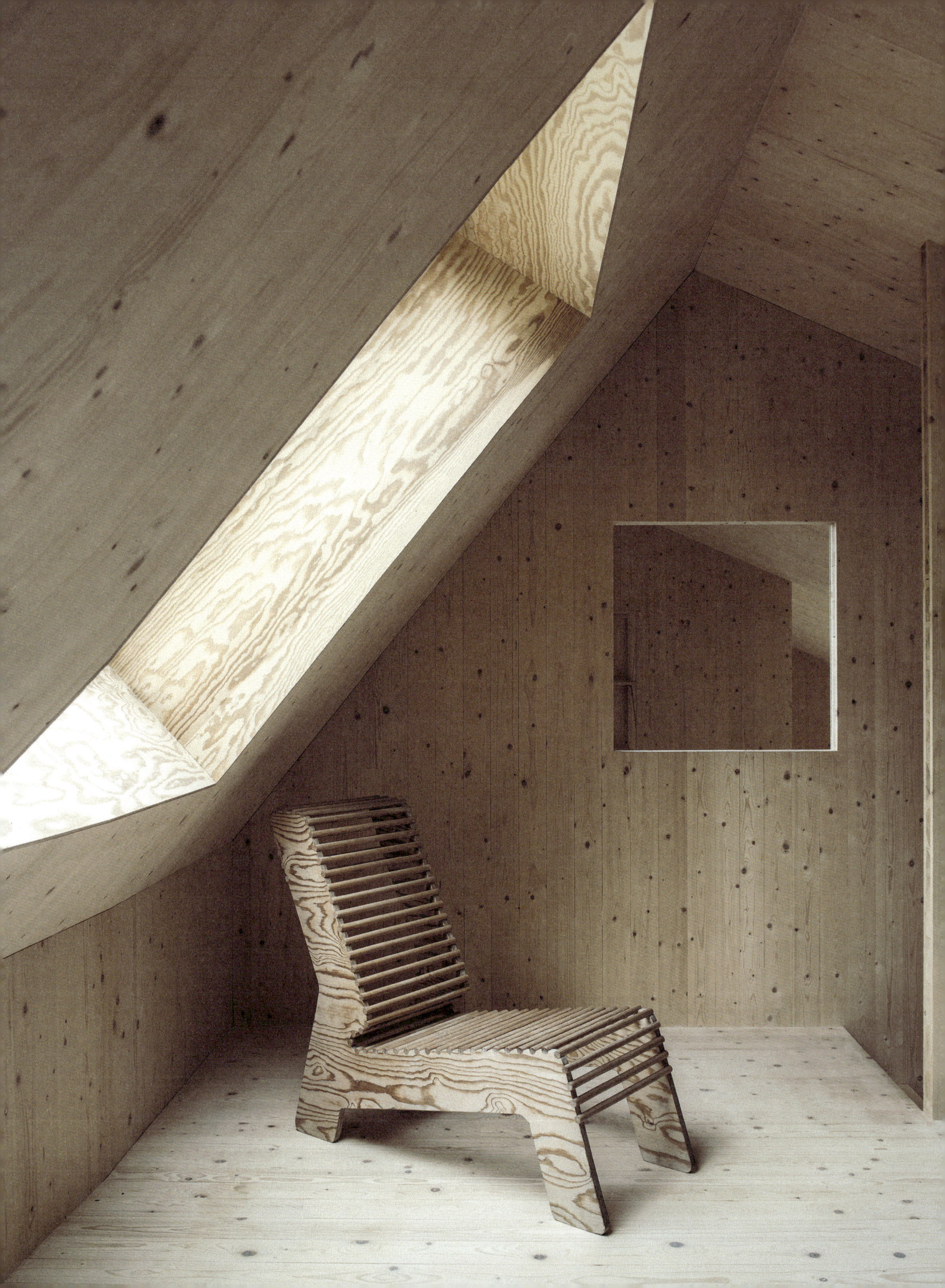

Inside, certain shapes are repeated, which is typical for TAF. The sliding window shutters have a cross motif that can also be seen on the little cabinet hanging on the right. To the left: The chairs are one of Gustafson's first creations at Konstfack art and design school in Stockholm.

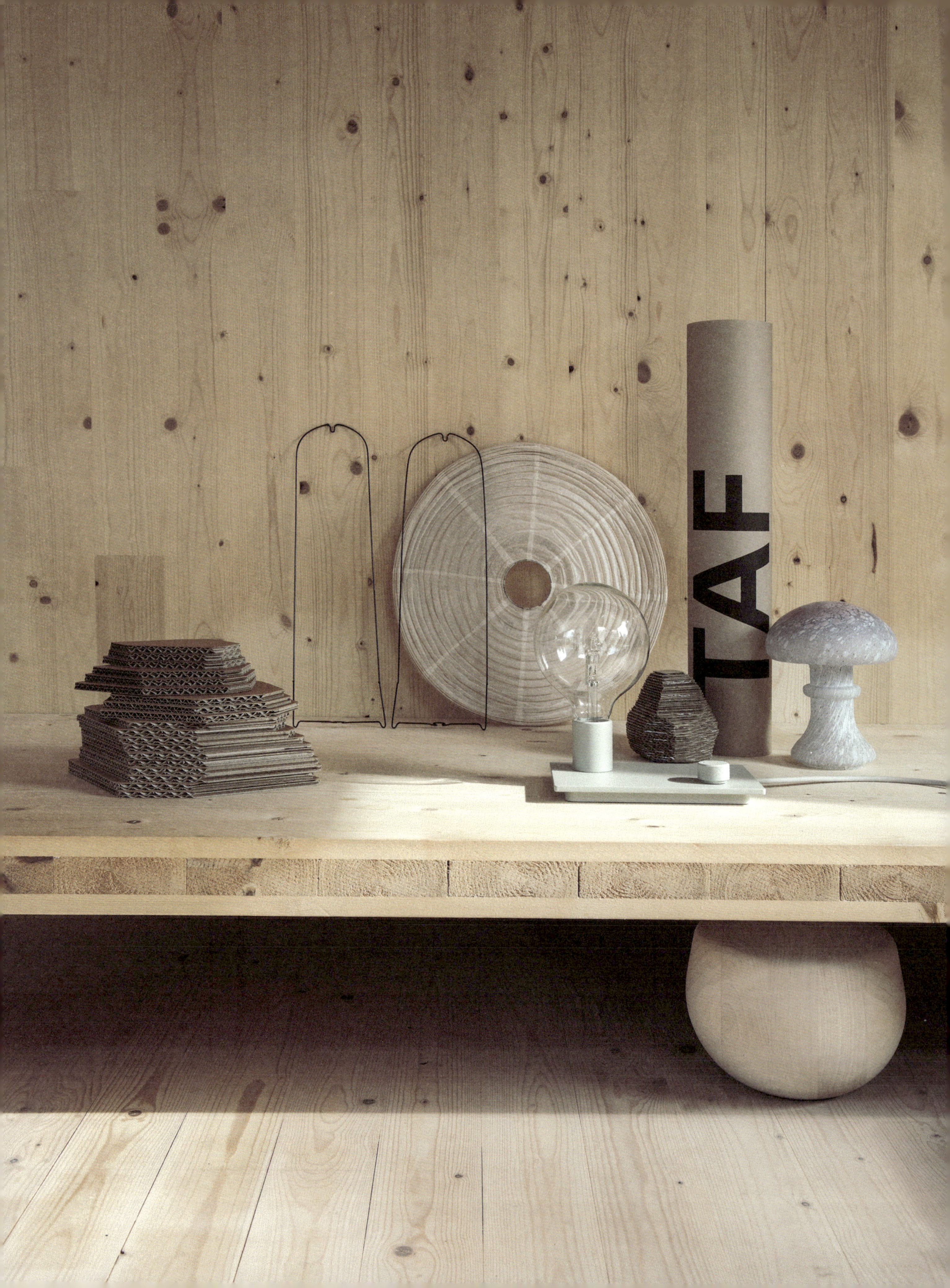
TAF

A simple kitchen solution. The Ambient ceiling lamp was designed by TAF for Muuto. The table and chairs were previously in Gustafson's parents' summerhouse. To the left: The bench was made from the same materials as the house's interior, and the leg is the same design as that used in TAF's small side tables. On the bench is the Control lamp from Muuto.

THE IMPORTANCE OF SPACE

How can we communicate our values in a spatial experience? Hugo Macdonald explores the rise of the well-designed branded space.

ONCE UPON A TIME, not so long ago, the idea of a brand was expressed primarily by a logo and a tagline. A brand was literally an image to be recognised visually, and a catchphrase to be heard and recited. It was splashed across billboards and merchandise; commercial entities vying for our attention and money. We bought into brands and became part of their gang.

Today we are more complex creatures, making sense, quietly and desperately, of a more complex world. We respond to values. We place importance on integrity.

We like to know where things come from, how they are made and that no one else has been squeezed or violated to bring them into being. Commerce has become more transparent, and hence more cultured as a result. A key consequence of this shift is the rise of the branded interior, and the development in our understanding of what a brand means today: it is a feeling and an experience, more than a superficial image or marketing tool.

From shops to offices, hotels to homes, and all the public-private and private-public spaces in between, we are experiencing spaces that have brand communication written into their interior make up. It's not to say that every surface has a logo on it. It's a subtler, more softly spoken but more strongly felt form of communication that matches our quest for brands to be holistic, trustworthy and coherent. A branded interior starts with the question: how can we communicate our values in a spatial experience? What do our values feel like as a sensory experience, not just to look at, but to touch, to hear, to smell and even taste?

Given that we largely still associate brands with commerce, retail design is at the frontline of this shift. We are all familiar with the game changer (to borrow the company's own expression) of Apple's temples of physical retail. It's hard, even just a decade later, to remember how confident it seemed to open a giant flagship with no logos inside, and instead to rely on a simple palette of natural materials (wood, stone and glass) and a layout that enabled sales staff to interact with customers over the products, not over a counter. It didn't just feel like stepping into an iPod, it felt like stepping into a worldview, and it spoke volumes. It was as if the mist had lifted, and suddenly it was obvious to everyone that an environment in which staff, customer and product come together should support and complete the experience as a vital touch point, not a pinch point.

I have often wondered if Steve Jobs and the retail architects at Eight Inc., who brought the Apple store concept to life, had visited Svenskt Tenn in Stockholm. The scale of operation and typology of product could not be further apart of course, but the effect of the experience is identical. As with Apple, when you step into Svenskt Tenn you are stepping into Estrid Ericson's world. You do not need to know Ericson or Josef Frank's story to feel the values at the heart of the company, values that have been carefully maintained and considerately updated for new audiences over almost a century. It is warm, crafted and alive. There is an acute sense of discovery. The knowledge, care and attention to detail is confidently transmitted in every fibre of the shop and brought to life by the wonderful people who work there. It is surely one of the most successful, enduring examples of a branded retail interior in existence. It was not dreamt up in a marketing boardroom. It was born from the vision and values, life and style of a real person: the ultimate lifestyle brand.

Today you cannot move for concept stores that have mapped

the successful formula of Apple and Svenskt Tenn to their own worlds, with varying degrees of success. The Artek store in Helsinki is a poetic evocation of Alvar Aalto's vision that has made sense of modern Finland and contemporary Finnish design; it is not a museum, it is a living, breathing experience that communicates so much more than the price of furniture. Oliver Gustav's emporium outside Copenhagen has quickly become a pilgrimage site for the design community. It is not a shop or a gallery, or even a concept store, but an inhabited world that touches all who visit. Gustav's skill has been to see beyond aesthetics and create a sensory environment that communicates a feeling. He understands that the sum of coherent curation is greater than its individual component parts, and the result is interior alchemy.

The potential of branded space reaches far beyond retail. As the boundaries of work and personal life are increasingly blurred, so too are the traditional templates for the design of our working spaces. Gone are the Taylorist principles of the office as a human factory for concentrated output. Now it's about creating working environments that encourage productivity in a more humane capacity. Our best workplaces today take the wellbeing of their occupants seriously, understanding that a healthy workforce is a happy, loyal and productive one. More than this, a workplace that is designed around its brand values communicates capability and intent, implicitly and explicitly. It gives employees something to belong to, to feel part of and invested in. It gives visitors and clients a tangible understanding of who the business is, beyond what they do and what they say.

I am fortunate to have worked with two pioneers in this realm. At *Monocle*, our headquarters at Midori House in London were an important tool in establishing and communicating the values of the magazine and media company. We would host visitors and clients from around the world, who could instantly see and feel that the editorial principles were matched by the working environment. Guests believed in the mission and the business because they could experience it for themselves – the messages within the magazine and the environment of the workspace were unequivocally aligned and made sense.

In the world of design, branded interior life is critical for helping people to understand that design is more than an aesthetic. At Ilse Crawford's studio, the principles of her philosophy have been embedded in the design of her headquarters, which has wellbeing at its heart. When people visit, they understand not just the skill of the studio and the working process, but importantly the values too; more than a look, it is a feeling, and a feeling that can only truly be communicated by first-hand experience.

Lotta Agaton's expanding design consultancy bears testament to this. Her studio is much more than a workplace, it is a living portfolio, where clients can feel, smell and hear her vision. The importance of acknowledging feeling in interior space, and recognising the benefits of extending brand into atmosphere, is gradually becoming mainstream. It's not a cynical ploy by marketing departments – it is part of the shift towards greater transparency in daily life, which can only be a good thing. You can create a fantasy in an interior, but you cannot easily communicate a lie. Interior experiences are hard to hide behind because they speak to us on more primal levels than simple logos and slogans. Consider the fast food chain that claims it cares for the health and wellbeing of its diners, but serves food in a dirty, institutional, dehumanising environment. It's a hard message to swallow.

By Hugo Macdonald

"IN THE WORLD OF DESIGN, BRANDED INTERIOR LIFE IS CRITICAL FOR HELPING PEOPLE TO UNDERSTAND THAT DESIGN IS MORE THAN AN AESTHETIC."

Lotta Agaton has been working as a stylist for more than 20 years and is one of Sweden's most renowned within the profession. She recently expanded her business from styling into interior design and moved into a studio at Kungsholmsstrand in Stockholm.

A place that talks
LOTTA AGATON

FOR SOMEONE WHO has largely defined and shaped the image of the Scandinavian interior over the past two decades, it is a surprise to hear Lotta Agaton say that she is shy. "When I started out as a stylist 20 years ago, the role of the stylist was anonymous and that suited me," she says. "Today everyone wants to be their own brand. So many younger people want to be a celebrity." A reluctant star perhaps, Agaton has recently expanded her business from styling into interior design – Lotta Agaton Interiors – and moved into a dedicated studio space in Stockholm's Kungsholmsstrand.

The move from styling (which she will continue to do) into interiors has been a holistic progression for Agaton. In part it was a response to frequent enquiries about whether she might do interior concepts for private residential and larger developments. But it also felt like a natural shift in her feelings towards design. "It feels more permanent," she says. "It's much slower than styling, where it's often about communicating ideas and fixing things quickly. I love the process of getting to know a client and then inhabiting their world, or imagining a world for a concept where there is no client."

Agaton's studio is her world, and it's easy to understand what an important tool it is for her in communicating not just the look, but the feeling of her work. "I always aim for an atmosphere, an ambience and a feeling," she explains. "It's hard to convey properly in a photograph, but when visitors come here, they understand. They touch, they feel, they smell, we talk. It's the most important part of building a relationship together."

It is visually striking, but the feeling is what is most memorable: it is ethereal, soothing, sensual and grounding. "I love to mix materials and textures, and I generally like to use one colour at a time, starting with a neutral base and building it up from there," says Agaton, describing her working process. The layered palette of materials, textures and colours lends the studio a compelling richness. There are surprising moments of nature – found objects that fit into the scheme perfectly. "I'm moved by structures in nature," she says. "Everything starts and comes back to this – the real colours of nature are the most beautiful."

Agaton is often described as a trendsetter, but her work appeals to something more primal and timeless than fashion. "I really don't like the word trend," she says. "I think people confuse it with mood. I'm curious and am always interested in finding new materials, colours, textures and applications. I'm interested in how changing politics and culture affect the way we feel and consequently what feels good to wear on our bodies and in our homes. This is how taste or trends change. It's something much more complicated than just deciding you suddenly like blue."

PHOTOGRAPHY: ERIK LEFVANDER STYLING: LOTTA AGATON

LOTTA AGATON | MY RESIDENCE 65

The sculpture is by Agaton's friend Staffan Bergquist. The curtains are made from Astrid fabric. To the right: The Quilt sofa is from Gärsnäs, the Crown chairs are from Massproductions and the vintage table is by Eero Saarinen.

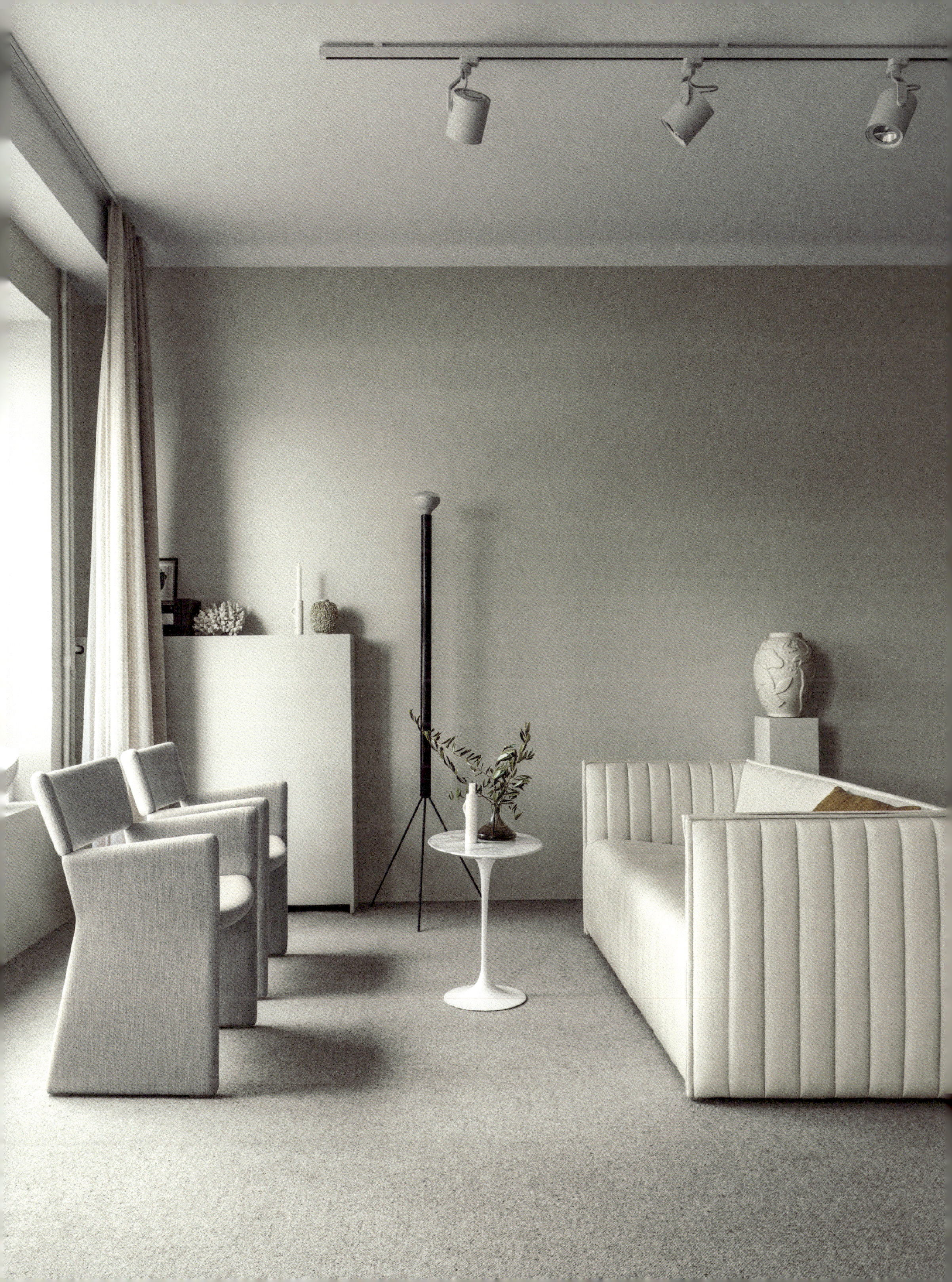

All the walls are covered with plaster from Kabe Copenhagen. Handbasin from Alape, faucet from Dornbracht and lamp from Wästberg. To the right: A conference table by Achille Castiglioni that was previously in the office of Agaton's father, who is an architect. Office chairs from Arper.

We are living at a time when design is becoming homogenised, and even bastardised. No sooner is something photographed than the space is reduced to just an image, which is then shared, posted, pinned and mood-boarded, with little consideration for the culture or context in which it might have been created. It's a shift that Agaton is acutely aware of. "Everything is so over exposed and it happens so quickly," she says. "You finish an interior and it's all over Pinterest. Suddenly it doesn't feel like your project any more. This is why it's so important to design places that have feeling, interiors that capture a mood in person, more than pictures. They are sacred and personal." For someone who is shy, you might imagine this is a difficult thing to communicate to clients in person, but Agaton has the answer. "This is what my studio is for," she says. "It's a place to tell people who I am and what I do, without me having to tell them myself."

By Hugo Macdonald

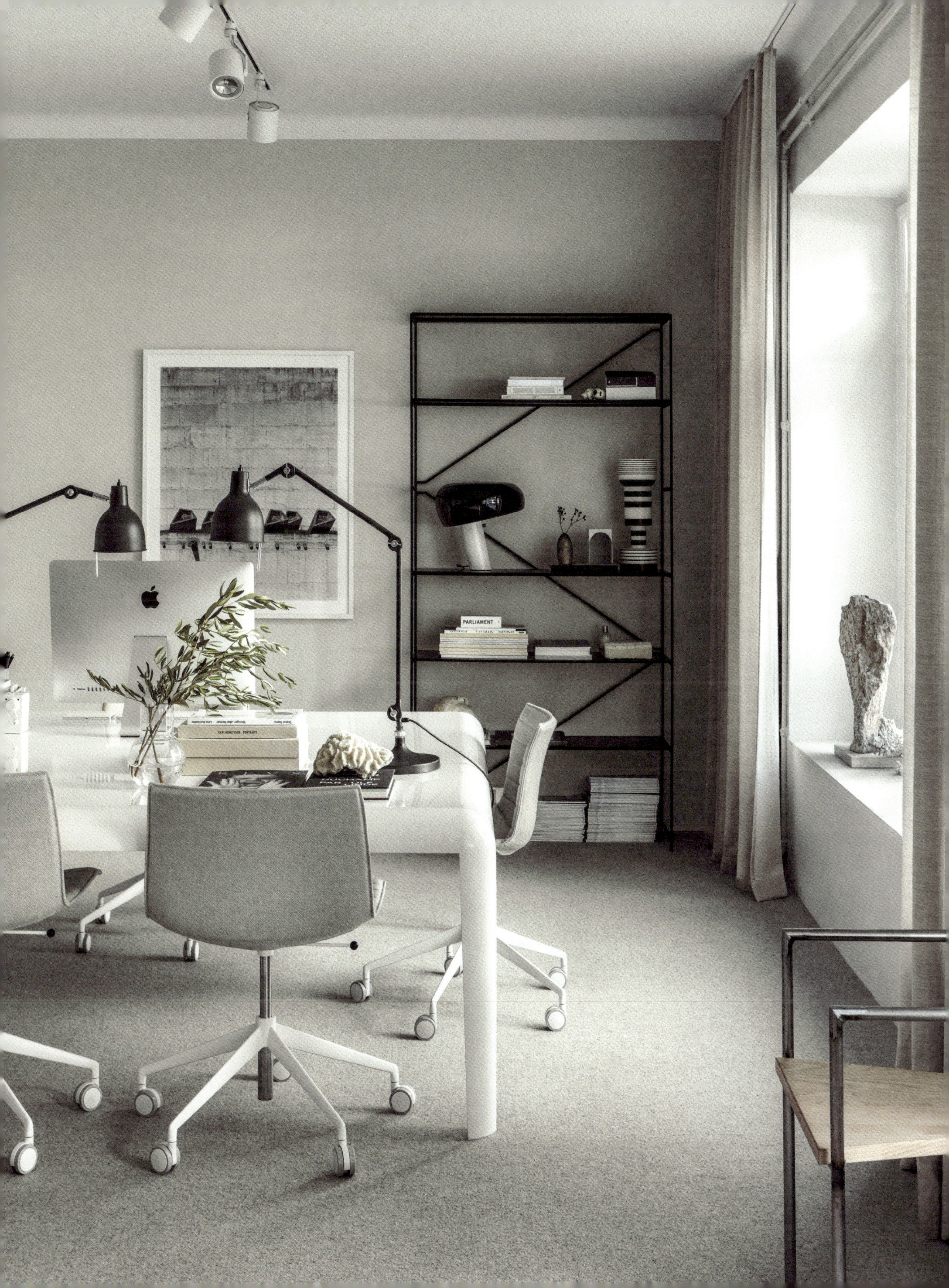
PARLIAMENT

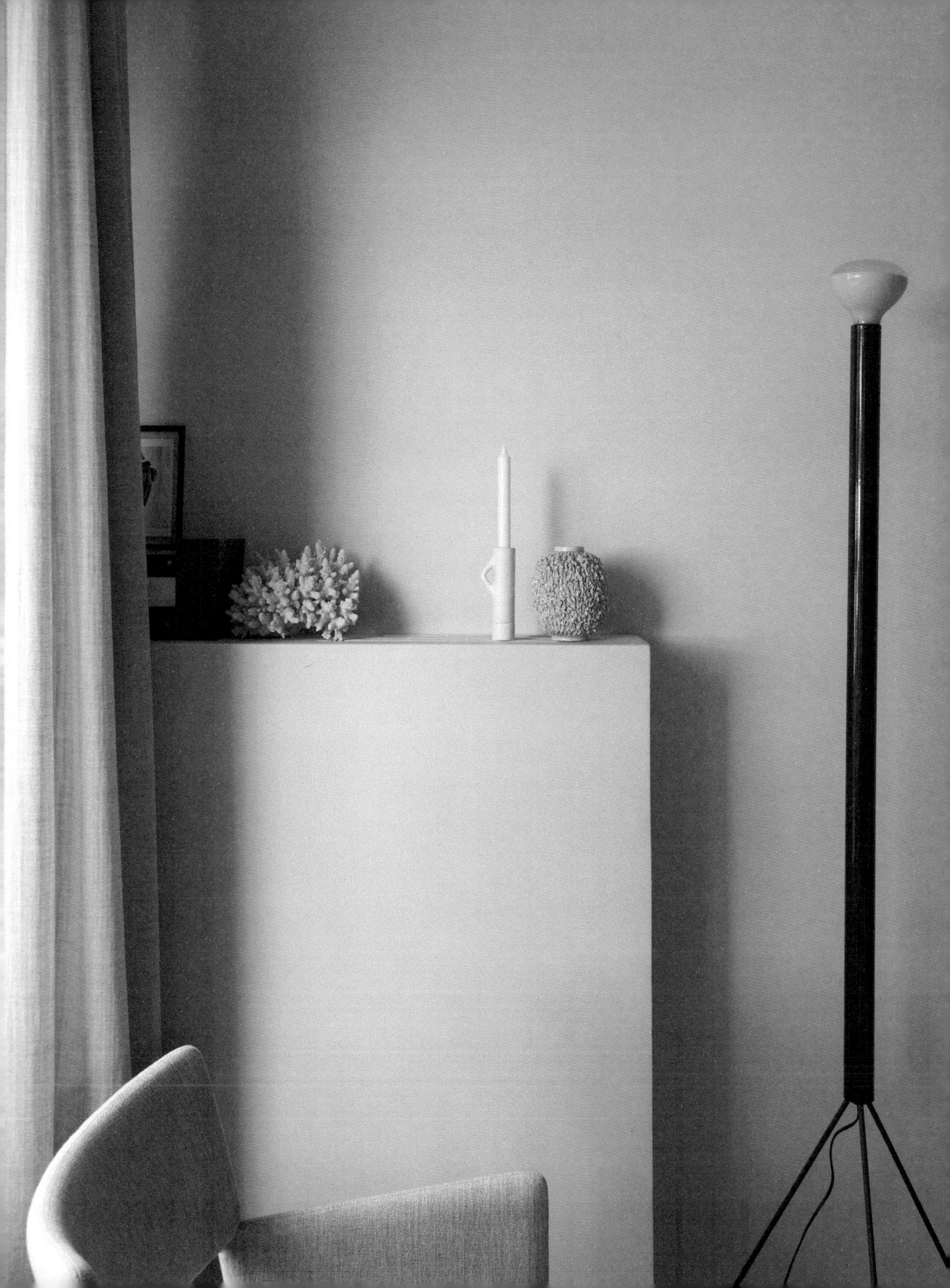

The shelf is from De Padova; with a lamp by Flos and a striped vase by Ettore Sottsass.
To the right: The cabinet attached to the wall was designed by Agaton for Picky Living. It is made from Douglas fir by Dinesen, and will be in production at the end of the year. On top of it is an artwork by Åsa Stenerhag, a concrete lamp by studio Viaduct and a speaker from Teenage Engineering. To the left: Floor lamp, a classic by Flos.

"THIS IS WHAT MY STUDIO IS FOR. IT'S A PLACE TO TELL PEOPLE WHO I AM AND WHAT I DO, WITHOUT ME HAVING TO TELL THEM MYSELF."

Hanna Wessman and Louise Liljencrantz are two of Sweden's most influential interior designers. Together they have recently acquired an office and studio in central Stockholm and have designed the interior with the same precision as the homes they work on for their clients.

A space to work
HANNA WESSMAN & LOUISE LILJENCRANTZ

HANNA WESSMAN AND Louise Liljencrantz are two of Sweden's most influential interior designers. Together they have acquired an office and studio space in central Stockholm and have designed the interior with the same precision as the homes they work on for their clients. Wessman is known for her popular blog Hanna's Room and as the interior designer for Sweden's best known television show about home improvement, *Äntligen hemma*. She also runs an online shop selling design products, as well as giving lectures and working as an interior designer for private clients. Louise Liljencrantz, who launched furniture brand Rood with Wessman last year, has in just a few years emerged as one of the most talked-about interior designers in Sweden.

"We would like to open the doors to creative meetings with artists, architects, suppliers and designers at our place," says Liljencrantz. "We want to create a place where we can inspire and get inspired by thoughts, ideas and contacts." Wessman agrees. "We have designed our office so that it may be used in many different ways, and maybe it could even be of interest for other brands, to host events in, do a photography shoot in or use as a pop-up showroom," she says. "We can even have a sit-down dinner for up to 15 guests. Today it feels important that office spaces are flexible and capable of multiple uses, but also that they represent the identity of the brand working there."

You have the furniture brand Rood together, but otherwise you have your own businesses. Why did you decide to get an office together?

Wessman: "It's both lonely and expensive to have this kind of business on your own. The ability to do something out of the ordinary is also greater when there are more of us sharing the costs."

Were you in agreement on how you wanted to decorate the premises?

Wessman: "Our starting point was how the space was going to be used and then we painlessly arrived at the design. We both need a lot of storage and quite a large table for presentations, colour decisions, creative meetings and workshops. The premises are divided into a larger and a smaller room, a kitchen and a lavatory. Our large table and most of the storage wound up in the bigger room and the smaller space became an office."

What was the inspiration for the interior design?

Wessman: "We've had the working name 'The Shop' all along, which I guess pretty clearly shows where we sought inspiration."

Liljencrantz: "The feeling we wanted to achieve was subtle, elegant and simple. We chose to work with light-coloured materials since the office faces north. Oak, steel and white are used throughout the premises. Hanna loves pink so the kitchen got salmon cabinet fronts and a terrazzo floor."

What needs did the premises have to satisfy?

Wessman: "The storage part is the most important, since both of us have quite a lot of material samples, from textiles to tiles and stone, which we would like to stow away. The large table for stylish and practical presentations with excellent lighting was also a necessity. This avoids us having to sit on our knees on the floor to cobble

PHOTOGRAPHY: ERIK LEFVANDER

HANNA WESSMAN & LOUISE LILJENCRANTZ | MY RESIDENCE 73

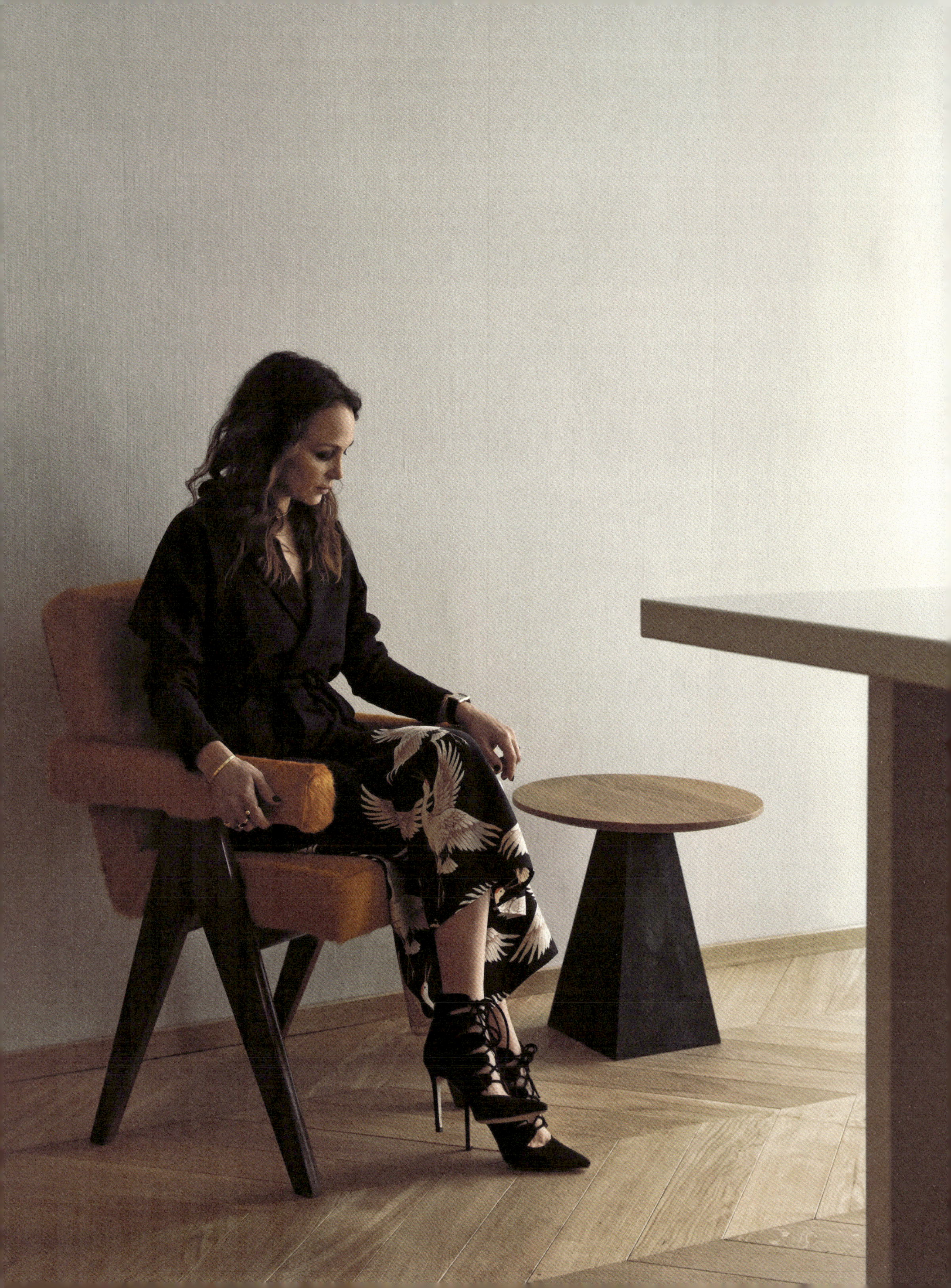

Wessman and Liljencrantz have used a similar colour scheme and materials in their office as those they often suggest for clients. The walls have cream-coloured linen wallpaper and the floor has French herringbone parquet. The alcoves have been covered in metal to create a sharper and more dramatic impression. To the left: The side table was designed by Liljencrantz with collaboration with carpenters Kfk, from their series Seed.

our concepts together. In addition, the interior design had to exude quality in order to represent our business in the best possible way."

Will the premises look like they do now or is this a work in progress?

Liljencrantz: "To be able to change the premises in a less costly way, we decided from the outset what could be replaced and what could not. The replaceable parts are the wall-to-wall carpet in the office section, the drapes towards the kitchen and the laminated screens in the windows. As an example, they can be covered in new laminate, textiles or can even be painted."

What has the response been like?

Wessman: "Our clients love it! The materials we use in our interior design assignments are the ones we have chosen for our studio, such as linen wallpaper and systems for electricity and sound. It is very constructive to be able to show on site what they look like and how they feel. Passers-by tell us that it is beautiful and inspiring and many people wonder if it's a shop."

Liljencrantz: "Many give us a thumbs up and a big smile, others stop and snap a picture. Even people who live in the area appreciate it; we have been told it is an improvement for the entire neighbourhood. And of course it means a lot to our clients to be able to see who we are and what we can do."

By Michelle Meadows

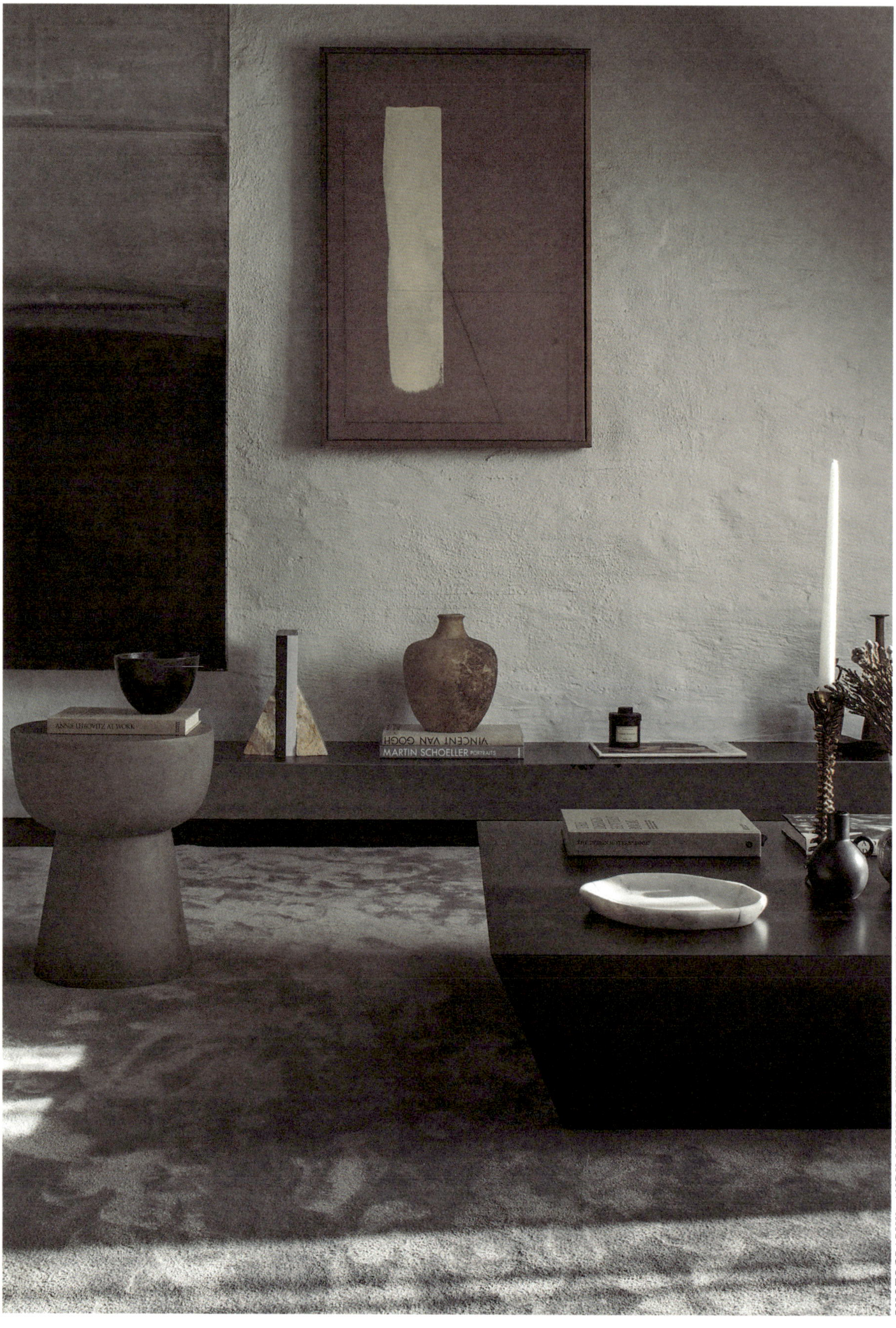

PHOTOGRAPHY: ANDY LIFFNER STYLING: HANNA WESSMAN

When the Swedish singer Måns Zelmerlöw was redesigning his flat, he contacted one of Sweden's most prominent interior designers, Hanna Wessman. They started with the kitchen and then took on the rest of the flat room by room. Zelmerlöw, who is currently writing music full time, is planning to move with his fiancée to England and wants Wessman to come and decorate the house there too.

Dreaming big
MÅNS ZELMERLÖW

THE SWEDISH SINGER-SONGWRITER Måns Zelmerlöw is not a man of small gestures. When he does something it has a tendency to get noticed. His musical career has led to several number one hits both in Sweden and abroad. He has hosted one of Sweden's biggest television shows, as well as winning the Eurovision Song Contest a couple of years ago with the widest margin of victory in the history of the competition. How does a person like that go about designing his own home?

"It's a lot easier for me to see the big picture than to focus on the smaller details," says Zelmerlöw. "When I walk into a house I can see what walls can be taken down and what could be built. I consider myself to be rather handy but that finds more of an expression at my summer place. I haven't dared to go wild as much in this place. It's a lot of fun to build cement walls for the kitchen, but it's easier at the country place with larger spaces to mess around in." This is why he got in touch with the equally dynamic interior designer Hanna Wessman [read more about her on page 72] through a mutual friend to help redesign his flat.

"I realised that the old kitchen looked awful, tiles made by the devil, everything in pine… it was terrible," says Zelmerlöw. "Hanna understood right away what I liked and presented a suggestion for how I could redesign the kitchen. Then it just went on from there. Now we have done every room. The result is really fantastic."

The collaboration was productive from the get go, though the duo were not entirely in agreement on everything at the beginning. It was hardly surprising that the struggle between the musician and the interior designer was about what musical equipment was necessary for a living space. "My speakers had to go immediately," he says. "The instruments have passed through a needle's eye; my guitars are pretty nice, not too many, only three or four. I really wanted to have the whole wall at the entryway full of guitars and found out this was not possible. But the grand piano looks good so there was no beef that it could stay."

Music is Zelmerlöw's focus right now. He spends most of his time in Surrey, south of London, along with his fiancée, writing songs for his upcoming album. The ambition is to really break through in Europe. "When I got to do my first European tour, it was one of my biggest dreams come true – then I really began to feel something happening," he says. "Now I have started to build up an audience outside of Sweden as well. The dream is to become more established all around Europe, to go on even bigger tours as an artist and to start playing at arenas in Europe. France and Poland have been the best so far. The song 'Should've Gone Home' was released in French and it was the second most played single on French radio last year. Poland has been around for me since 2007 – when we returned there at the end of the last tour to Warsaw, it

"WHEN I WALK INTO A HOUSE I CAN SEE WHAT WALLS CAN BE TAKEN DOWN AND WHAT COULD BE BUILT."

Zelmerlöw, one of Sweden's best-known singers, is currently writing new material. The small side table next to him is from Zara Home. The small side table next to him is from Zara Home. To the left: The rug from Linoleumkompaniet has been adapted by Hanna Wessman. The sofa is from Posh Living and the daybed was designed by Wessman. The wooden chairs by Jean Prouvé are from Dusty Deco in Stockholm. The coffee table and shelf were designed by Wessman. The black lamp is by Serge Mouille. The art and pottery are from Dusty Deco.

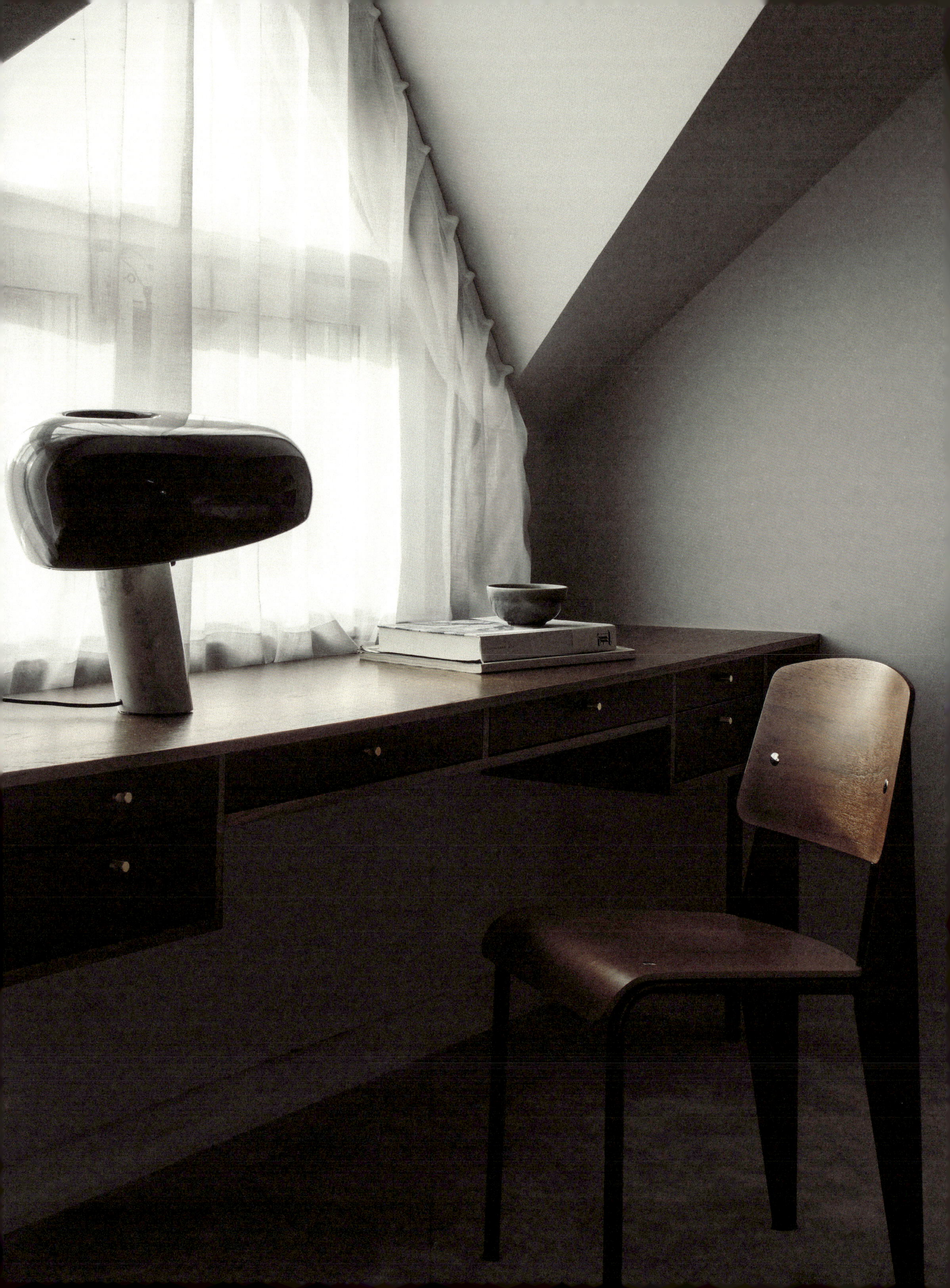

The bed is from Mille Notti and the bedside table is by Wessman. The lamp is from Garbo Interiors. The small side table is from Zara Home. To the left: The custom-built desk was designed by Wessman. The chair is by Jean Prouvé and the Snoopy lamp is from Flos.

was the first time I had done a real show in Poland in seven or eight years. When we got there the whole crowd had printed signs that read 'Welcome Home'."

Zelmerlöw is currently making plans to move to England full time with his fiancée and her child. But it's still a bit too early for him to pick up the speakers from the cellar. "I've split my time for a while now," he says. "Right now I'm in Surrey and writing most of the time – I'm so happy just going down to the studio and tinkering with songs. But the plan is to move there, at least for a few years. It's nice that it's a bit outside of London so you can decide when you want to go into town and when you want to stay in the countryside with the garden and the dogs. But when I move there, I obviously want Hanna to come along and help out with the interior decorating."

By Tom Cehlin Magnusson

Artists Hertha and Gösta Hillfon's fairy-tale home on the outskirts of Stockholm affected everyone who visited it. A few years after Hertha's death in 2013 the house was sold, but we had the privilege to take one last look before the objects were scattered to various locations. Anyone who wishes to get a taste of Hertha's magnificent oeuvre can visit the museum created in her name at Skeppsholmen in central Stockholm.

A creative cosmos
HERTHA & GÖSTA HILLFON

A HOUSE WITHOUT people is not a home. When Swedish ceramic artist Hertha Hillfon died in the autumn of 2013 at the age of 92, her home and studio in the Stockholm suburb of Mälarhöjden was left vacant after 70 years of work. Under whispering trees amidst a solid community of family houses was one of Sweden's finest artist residences. It had been photographed and written about extensively, but now there was a poignant emptiness and an uncertain future. In Sweden, many studios remain as legacies of their grand masters, among them Carl Milles, Anders Zorn, Carl Larsson and Carl Eldh, but sadly few female artists' studios remain. We had the chance to visit Hillfon's magical place one spring day before the house was sold and the contents dispersed.

Without the presence of the artist herself, with her breakfast basket and black floppy hat, busily imparting aphorisms, the home echoes with a sacral stillness where myths and stories flourish. But from the shadows another voice also emerges, that of Gösta Hillfon, Hertha's husband, who died in 1995.

Gösta was an exhibition architect and artist, and the couple met in Stockholm at the art school of painter Edvin Ollers in 1939. When they were about to have their first child, they moved to Gösta's parents' property in Mälarhöjden, where there was a small summerhouse and cabin. During the first ten years, Hertha painted at home while Gösta worked at his father's sign manufacturing company. When the children had reached school age, Hertha applied to Konstfack in Stockholm, one of Sweden's foremost art schools, and found her calling in ceramics. Her bold sculptural works broke with the delicate design language of the 1950s and she quickly achieved a reputation as an innovator, a "baroque wildcat among pottery ermines", as one critic wrote. Her pottery was shown abroad, as evidence of the high quality of Swedish craft. In 1962 she received the prestigious Lunning Prize, seen as the Nobel Prize of design at the time. The larger world of public commissions opened up.

Gösta also achieved his breakthrough during these years as an exhibition architect, with a celebrated show about the city of Norrköping in 1964. At the end of the 1960s, Hertha had to start turning down

PHOTOGRAPHY: KARIN BJÖRKQUIST STYLING: JAKOB SOLGREN

The round window in the drawing cottage was given by friend and architect Bengt Lindroos. To the right: The wooden staircase looks almost as if it floats freely; here Hertha once fell and broke her arm. The bird of prey head is one of Hertha's sculptures in clay.

"HERTHA HILLFON'S BOLD SCULPTURAL WORKS BROKE WITH THE DELICATE DESIGN LANGUAGE OF THE 1950S AND SHE QUICKLY ACHIEVED A REPUTATION AS AN INNOVATOR, A 'BAROQUE WILDCAT AMONG POTTERY ERMINES'."

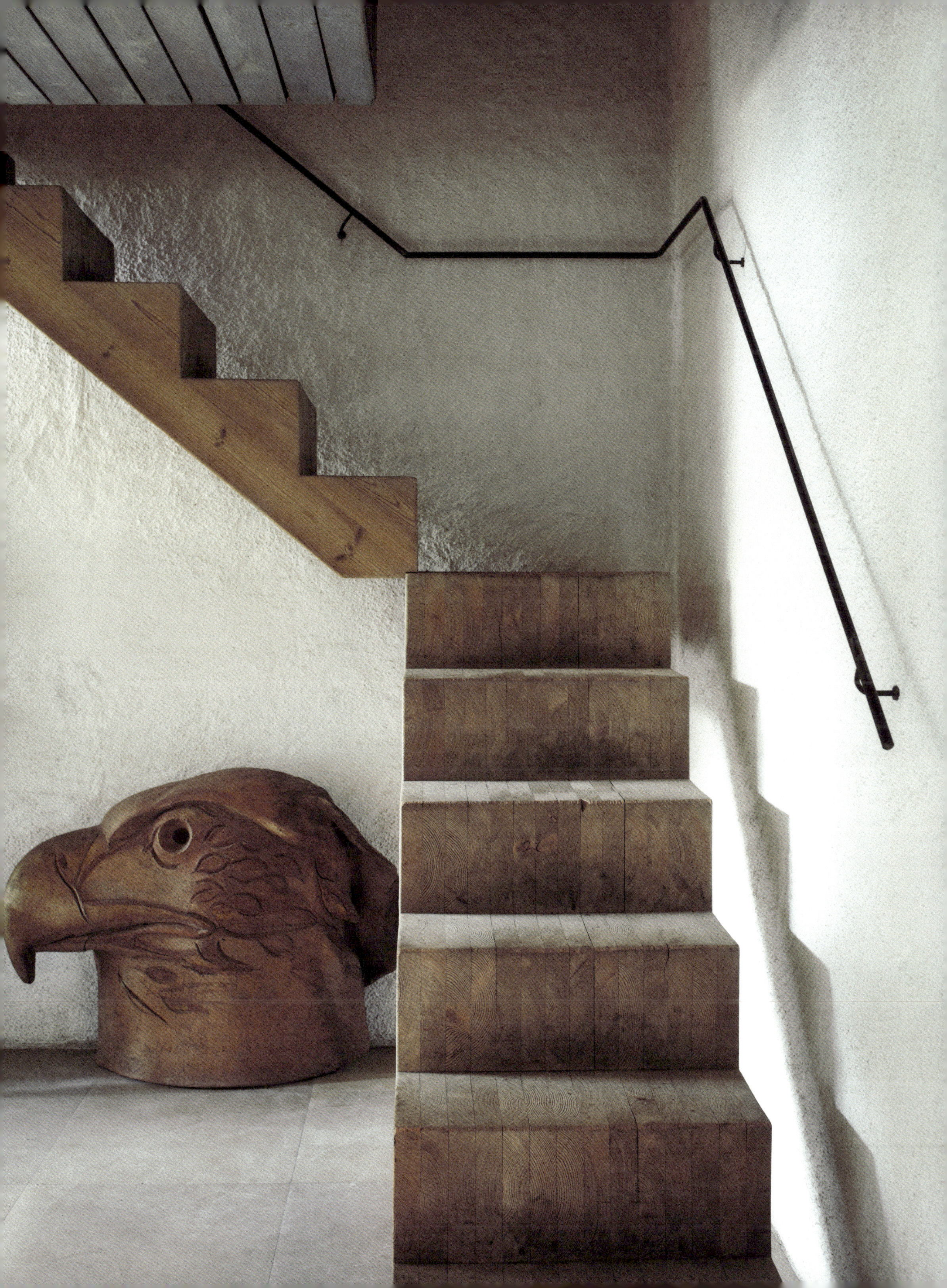

Hertha's creations were often large – the spacious studio was the place where she received her models and served coffee and ginger cookies. To the right: The kitchen was built in 1968 and was designed by Gösta Hillfon.

assignments because her studio was too small. At this point Gösta designed a new house, with lots of northern light and living quarters that still retain a timeless feel. A refined simplicity has kept the place alive. Today we might interpret the setting as Japanese influenced, but inspiration may well have come from Swedish folk culture, with solid materials reduced by Gösta's minimalist perfectionism: a slanted roof on lightweight concrete blocks, support walls in white stucco, unpainted wooden window frames, nailed wooden roof tiles and durable floorboards. Gösta's sense of proportion and how the light falls makes the simplest materials seem to float in perfect balance.

There was hope that the house and its contents could remain this way forever. But forgetfulness is quick and relentless, even around a legend like Hertha Hillfon. Perhaps in the end it is most beautiful to let everything be scattered by the wind, to become memories, as in one of her aphorisms: "A crushed bowl, a memory. Now I love the shards more."

By Tom Cehlin Magnusson

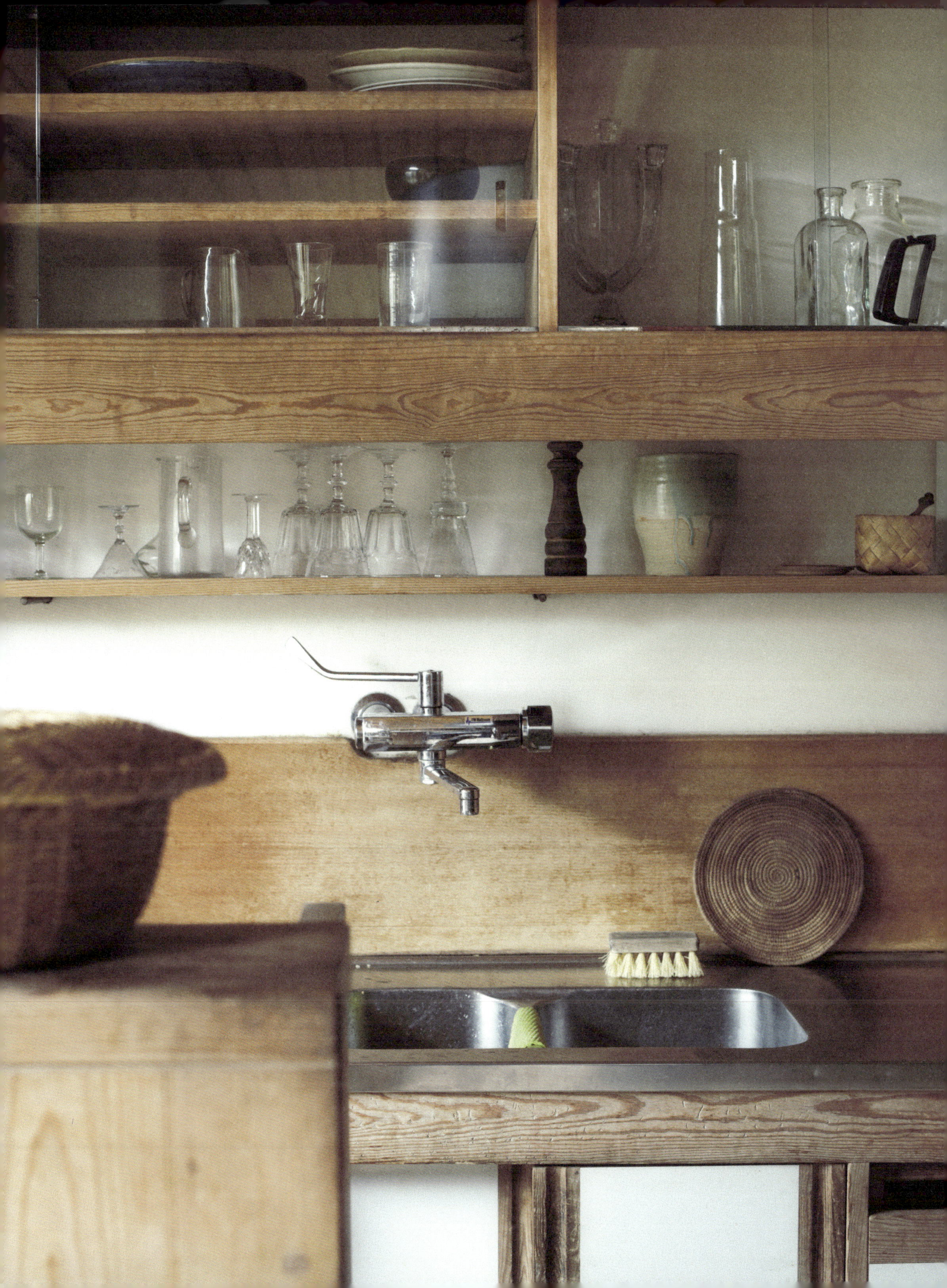

For more than three years photographer Bruno Ehrs documented the transformation of a military bunker into a piece of modern, iconic architecture. The private bunker is situated on the Swedish island of Gotland and is owned by Stefan Bengtsson, a Gotland enthusiast and grandson of H&M's founder Erling Persson.

PHOTOGRAPHY: BRUNO EHRS

BUNKER ONE ZERO FOUR

Swedish ptotographer Bruno Ehrs has captured the transformation of a forgotten military bunker into an unusual luxury residence.

SWEDISH PHOTOGRAPHER Bruno Ehrs' book *Bunker Ett Noll Fyra* (*Bunker One Zero Four*) depicts the transformation of a forgotten military bunker on Gotland, Sweden's largest island, into an outstandingly unusual residence, combining raw concrete with a vision of exquisite luxury. Architect Erik Gardell of local firm Skälsö Arkitekter led the reconstruction, inspired by the German bunkers of the Atlantic Wall in Normandy, northern France.

"The bunker was like a sculpture that immediately took hold of me," says Ehrs, who sees the work as an art project as much as an architectural one. The pictures have caught the attention of the media, including coverage in *Wallpaper** magazine in December 2016, as well as being exhibited at Gotlands Museum in Visby, on the west coast of Gotland, in summer 2017. Ehrs' photography project was not merely a work assignment, but very much his own artistic idea. "I just cared about what I thought was interesting – the seriousness, the play of lines, the proportions and beautiful surfaces and all the shades in the colourless below," he says. "The bunker was portrayed with a different vision to that of an architect. The photographer's eyes were the only ones to be advised." The book itself is as tactile and powerful as its subject.

Bungenäs in northeastern Gotland was once a windswept outpost with lime quarries and defunct bunkers to the east. The harsh nature and proximity to the sea attracted only bird watchers and the occasional romantic soul. Over the past decade, the promontory has become a hip residential paradise where Gotlanders move into the converted defence buildings for the summer. The largest of them is Bunker 104, built in 1937 over three floors underground, to resist shelling and bombs if the area were to be attacked. A more stolid and doleful building is hard to imagine. It is as much a James Bond-style location as a monument to the Cold War's

*Bunker 104 was completely hidden underground and for many years no one knew what was down there.
Today the property also includes two newly built houses above ground. All of the designs have their origins in military aesthetics,
and nearly everything, down to the last detail, has been specially made for the project.*

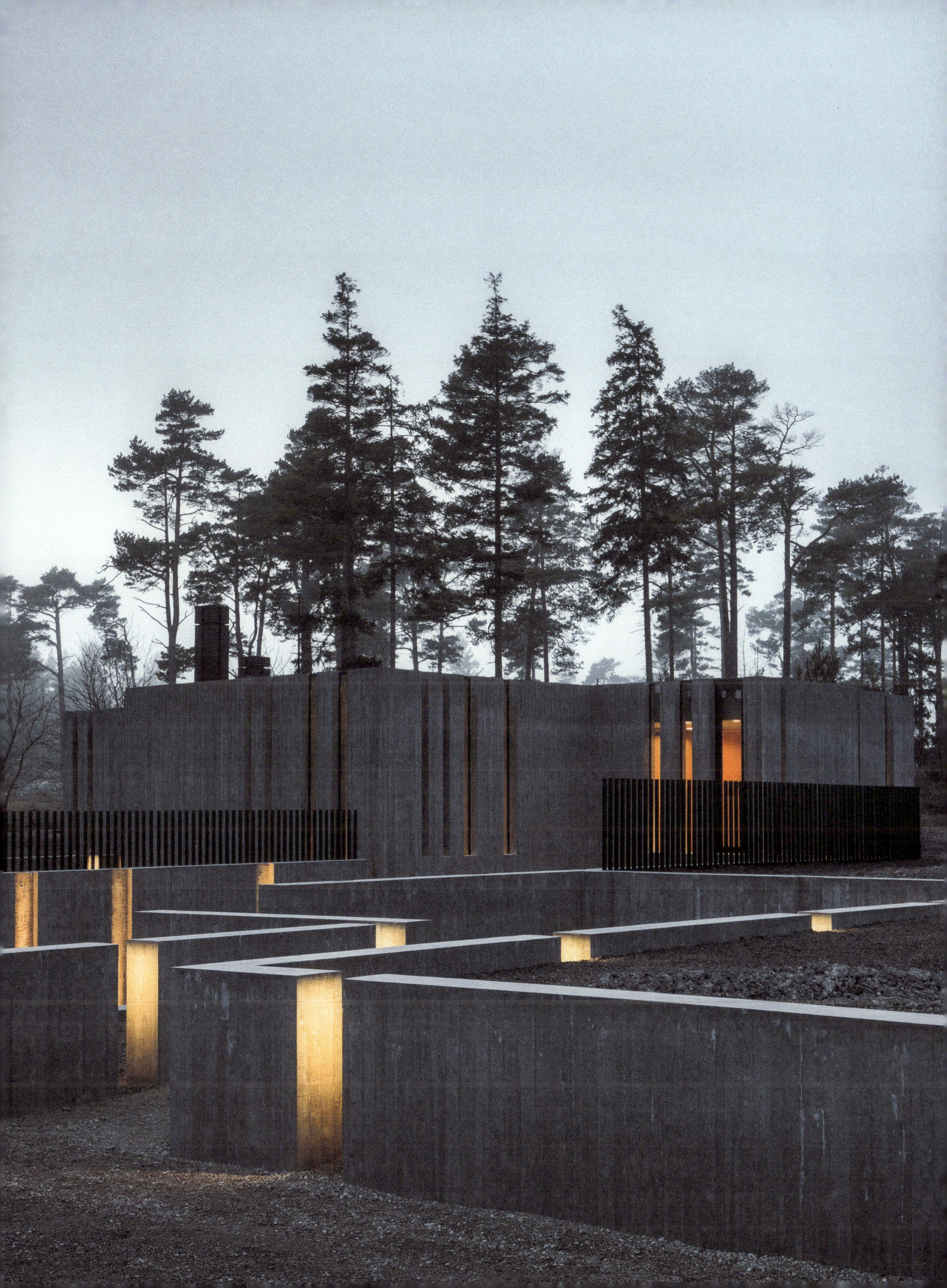

An early picture of the original bunker, where a layer of dirt has been removed and the military concrete construction is revealed. In the middle is the entrance to the stairway below ground level. To the right: Working with different types of light flow in this special building has been important.

defence faction, and the Gotland concrete industry. The bunker was abandoned and remained invisible, largely underground, until 2007. The complex was then bought by local entrepreneur Joachim Kuylenstierna, who in turn sold it on. The army had filled the entrance with a mass of rocks, so nobody could enter the building. Eventually the underground levels were made accessible and Ehrs made the descent, arriving just as the bunker was opened. "At that point I went down and stepped into a work of art," he says. "It was love at first glance, a feeling of both fear and delight. It smelled of diesel oil and brackish water, and a sense of threat blended with a longing to proceed further inwards." The bunker's gloomy beauty enchanted Ehrs, who over a period of three and a half years visited the bunker 17 times, the longest lasting 13 hours underground. He became increasingly fascinated by the new architecture that was emerging. "The artwork became even more refined," he says. Openings were made to let in light and gun ports became skylights. There was no attempt to soften the space – instead a harsh and dramatic beauty permeates the building. On the surface above, a new residential building was constructed, characterised by the bunker aesthetic. The jagged angles of the trenches informed the system of construction on the plot above.

"I'm looking for personal, not private," says Ehrs, who for the first year of the project didn't know who would buy the place and live here. "Bunker 104 will probably become an iconic piece in Swedish architectural history, such as Erik Gunnar Asplund's Villa Snellman or Josef Frank's Falsterbo villas. Above all, it is the boldness that impresses. What was built for war is now built for beauty."

By Petter Eklund

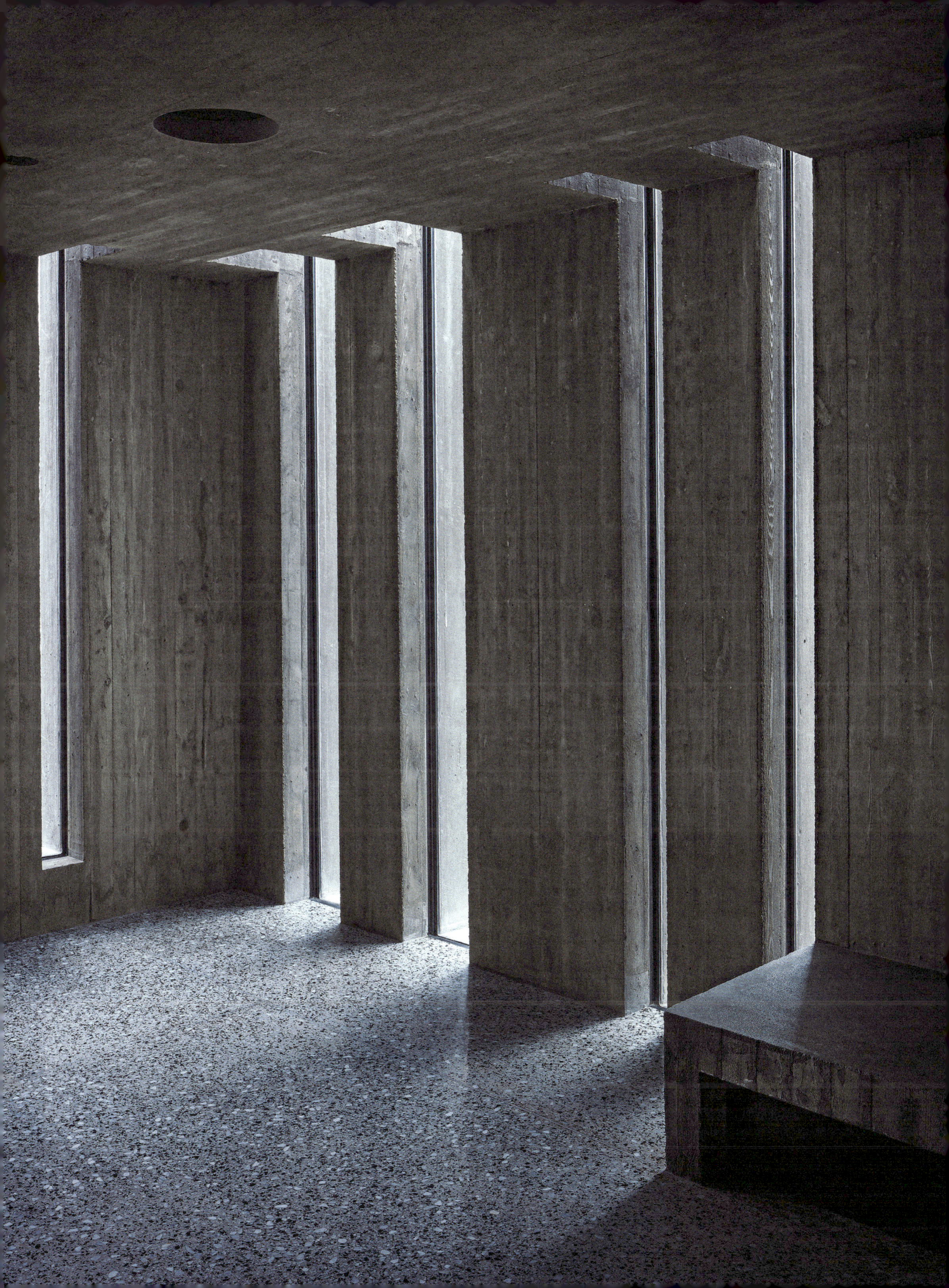

This extravagant project was developed as a summer home. The different buildings can be used separately if the owners have guests — there are, for example, three kitchens.

BJÄLKLAGET ÄR BERÄKNAT FÖR
EN BELASTNING AV 1000 KG/KVM

Erik Gardell on the Bungenäs site, where him and his colleagues at Skälsö Arkitekter created the zoning plan inspired by the Sea Ranch in California. The architects have been sensitive to the surrounding nature, not allowing the new houses to take up too much space so that the area does not become completely privatised.

SKÄLSÖ ARKITEKTER

The architects behind Sweden's most unusual summer village, Joel Phersson and Erik Gardell, on creating houses in a severe landscape.

SKÄLSÖ ARKITEKTER IS a young architectural firm that opened in connection with the development of the unique area of Bungenäs on the island of Gotland. The firm recently received *Residence Magazine's* Architect of the Year award.

Tell me about Bungenäs, your zoning plan and the design of it?

"The Bungenäs peninsula has acquired its special character from a variety of activities. Around 1906, the land was sold to the limestone industry, which soon began large-scale stone quarrying for industrial purposes. A few years later, the two limestone kilns were built, which still stand today as landmarks. By the mid 1960s, Bungenäs was Gotland's largest limestone quarry. Around the harbour, a small industrial community had developed, with a general store, residences for labourers and dining facilities. By 1963, the government considered Bungenäs to be of such great importance from a defensive point of view that the entire area was purchased. The area was fenced off and completely closed to the public, and was not opened until 2000, when the KA3 regiment in Fårösund was closed down.

In 2010, we received the assignment from the new property owner Joachim Kuylenstierna to devise a comprehensive zoning plan. The aim of the project was to create a new yet historically anchored layer of solid architecture without forsaking the history of the site. Approximately 120 plots fit into the plan. The historic buildings have been restored and the old fence that once kept the public outside the area remained in place, to prevent the entry of cars, and now visitors may enter on foot or by bike. The rare Gotland coastal vegetation is prevalent and is, of course, a vital part of the landscape. Any new add-ons are adapted to the location."

Instead of creating traditional houses, you have created something that hasn't been seen before – what references did you initially have?

"To begin with, it was the surrounding nature and historical layers that, in conjunction with the military's old buildings, made up the greatest source of inspiration for our architecture. Materials and designs tie into the site, and the buildings lie humbly between trees and rocks. The main construction reference for Bungenäs was the Sea Ranch in California, a couple of hours' drive north of San Francisco. That area is considerably older and larger, but shares many basic ideas with Bungenäs. For example, all additions must be adapted to their unique context, there is a strong focus on quality architecture, and development should take place prudently and over a long period of time."

How has the architecture affected the area and the surroundings?

"Today there are about 20 completed houses on Bungenäs. The intention with the plan for the area has been that the new houses should not take up too much space, so that the area does not become completely privatised. Even if all the plots are built upon, they only occupy about 10 per cent of the peninsula, allowing visitors to discover the area. A few years into the project, the area still feels open and largely untouched. What the new buildings all have in common is that they adapt to nature. Indoors and outdoors are fused together and the palette of materials is honest: wood is wood, concrete is concrete, we spackle and paint as little as possible."

Tell us about Bunker 104 and the adjoining building – how did the project develop?

"The idea of placing a plot above the bunker in the zoning plan was that it could be converted into a home. But we were taking a chance when we situated the plot, as nothing of the bunker was visible above ground. Bunker 104 was only known from old military drawings, and we saw a section of the underground construction that looked absolutely incredible. When we came to the site with our potential client for the first time, we only had the drawing. The project was born around the idea of a 14-metre-high underground room with a large skylight – a bit like a buried church hall."

For many, the idea of a secret underground bunker is quite scary. How is the bunker supposed to be used?

"Building 104, which is the military name of the place, represents the old part of the project, which now also includes two newly-built houses above ground. I would also have some doubts about living only underground, but now there are some features that are in the bunker below, while others are above ground."

Practically speaking, how was the bunker designed? With the military aspects as a starting point, what details had the greatest importance?

"The project is a summerhouse. The different bodies of houses can work separately, so there are, for example, three kitchens. Purely schematically, we started with the bunker and when we saw that the surface was not large enough and that we needed more space, it was natural for us to consider an extension. How do you build an addition to a bunker? Everything we have designed has its origins in our idea of the military. Of course it is rather romantic; a kitchen or shower nozzle can never be too utilitarian. Because of that, we have had almost everything specially made in the house."

By Hanna Nova Beatrice

Michelle Meadows is an editor at Residence Magazine. She also works as a film and television actress. Her apartment from 1882 is filled with unique furniture from around the world.

An actress with a sense of style
MICHELLE MEADOWS

NOT ONLY IS Michelle Meadows an editor at *Residence Magazine*, she also works as a film and television actress. Her portrayal of the cold, unhappy Eva in Johan Kling's critically acclaimed 2007 film *Darling* saw her nominated for best actress at the Swedish film industry's Guldbagge Awards.

Meadows spent the first years of her life in Los Angeles in the 1980s. Although she was mostly raised in Stockholm, she feels she is permanently living in the wrong climate zone. "You can sense my American years through my love of peanut butter, palm trees and warm temperatures," she says.

Meadows' apartment is situated in the heart of Stockholm's Södermalm district, where veganism is at its peak, with an organic fair-trade shop on every block. Cream-coloured walls, black leather sofas, golden palm trees, porcelain lions… it is obviously not the home of an ordinary Scandinavian. "I have found a lot of my things through my mother, who has lived in Bahrain, South Africa, Canada, Dubai, Spain, England and Iceland," says Meadows. "Some of the things you can find in stores in Stockholm too, but they have a special meaning for me."

Meadows' grandmother grew up in Stockholm and spent her weekends at legendary Stockholm clubs such as Nalen and Berns, and worked at the city's Gröna Lund amusement park. There she met an American, whom she married in the 1950s. Their son Michael travelled to Sweden at the beginning of the 1980s to study the history of ideas and hang out with his Swedish relatives. Somewhere along the line he met Meadows' mother.

Meadows has many different interests and hobbies, but two of the most important came at an early age. "As long as I can remember I have wanted to be an actress, and I have always loved interior design," she says. "That's why my two jobs, as an actress and a design journalist, are the perfect combination for me."

Her job at *Residence* has made her more aware of interior trends and has helped her develop her own style. "I like unique things with history and design that age well," she says. "I hardly ever buy anything new – my stuff is a combination of gifts, heirlooms or auction and thrift store finds."

Meadows has now decided it is time to move home. "I have lived in this apartment for the last ten years," she says. "It has been my happy place and the only place I have moved to freely. So it is a huge challenge to leave it, but at the same time it is a chance to clear up some of my hoarded stuff and insert new energy."

By Imke Janoschek

PHOTOGRAPHY: ANDY LIFFNER STYLING: THOMAS LINGSELL

MICHELLE MEADOWS | MY RESIDENCE 99

Raised in Los Angeles and Stockholm, Meadows loves leather sofas and palm tree lamps. To the right: In the kitchen, triangular candle holders from Dansk and 19th-century Swedish neo-renaissance chairs are combined with an old Chinese poster. The table was bought 16 years ago and now has a nice patina.

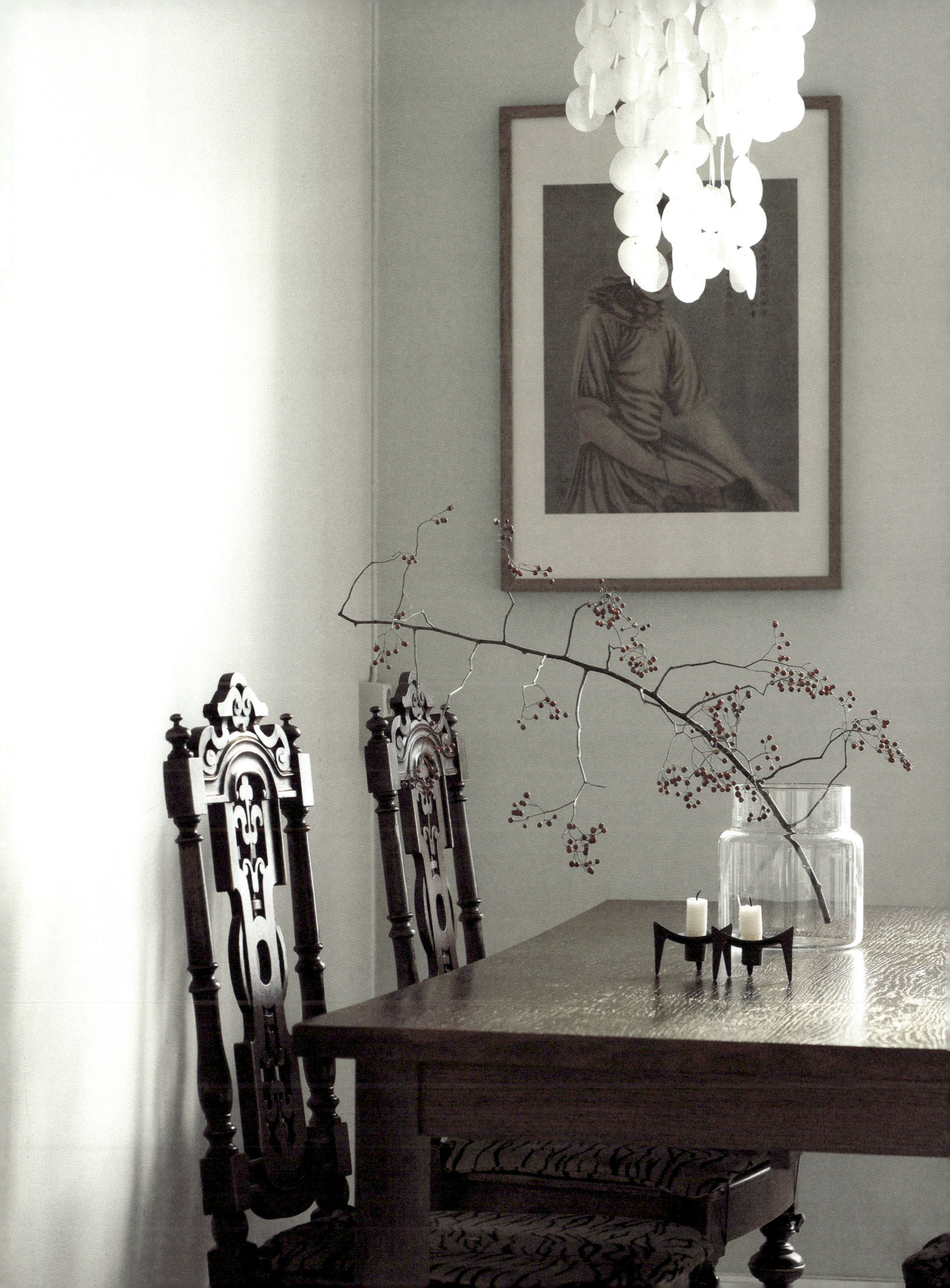

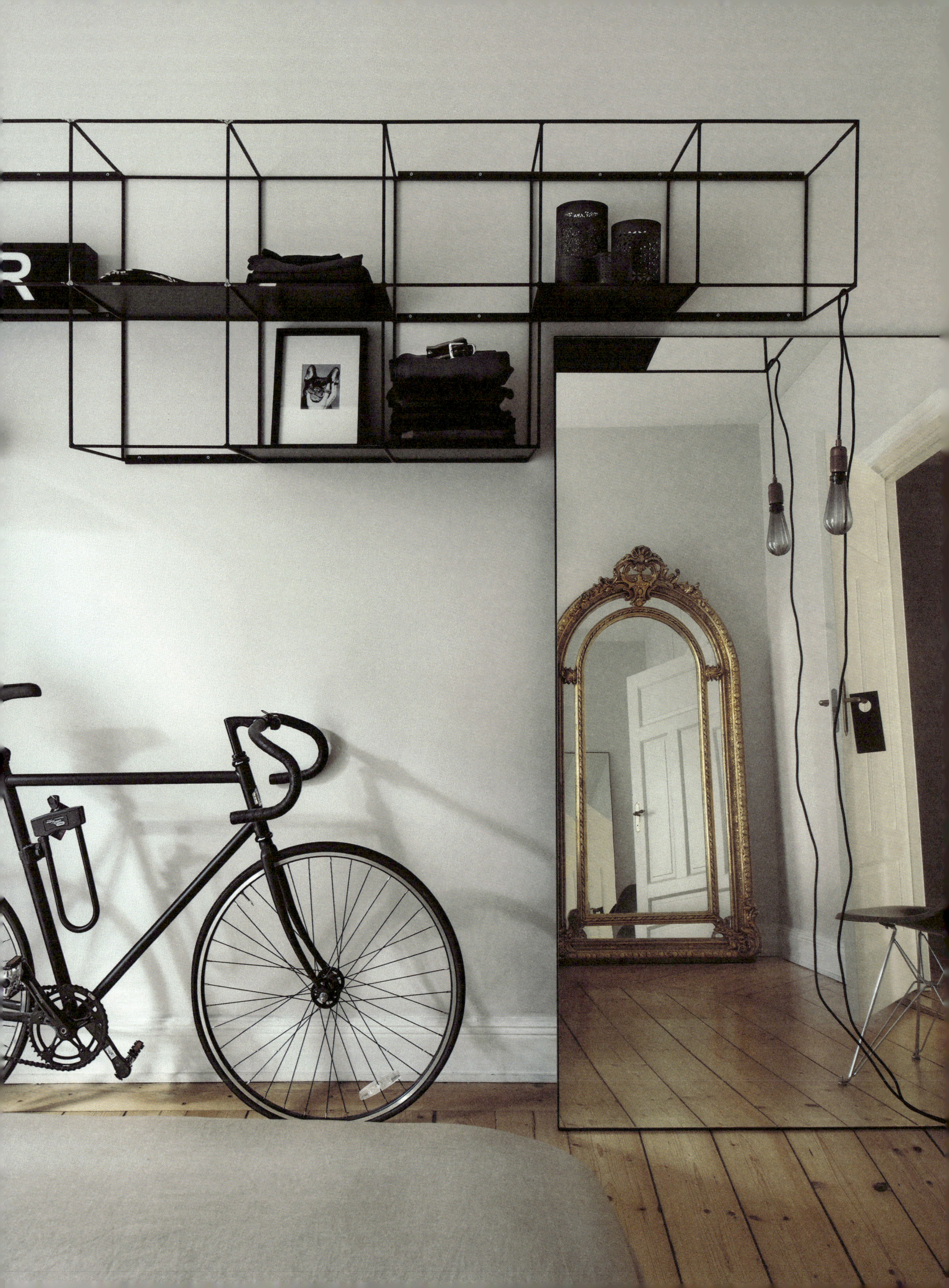

The door between the living and dining rooms is guarded by two porcelain lions that were once part of a fountain in a garden. To the left: The black mirror and shelf were originally made by Guise architects for V Ave Shoe Repair's flagship store in Stockholm.

MAGNUS WITTBJER & MICHA VAN DINTHER | MY RESIDENCE 104

PHOTOGRAPHY: ERIK LEFVANDER

Micha van Dinther is a design writer and art director, and Magnus Wittbjer is a copywriter and marketing strategist. They live in a 290-square-metre stone house from the 19th century in the village of Hunnestad, almost as far south as you can get in Sweden. Together they run online lifestyle store TypeO.

Quality of life
MAGNUS WITTBJER & MICHA VAN DINTHER

IT WAS A PERFECT summer day when they made up their minds. Magnus Wittbjer and Micha van Dinther were on holiday at Wittbjer's parents' summerhouse in France and were enjoying moving around freely inside as well as outside at their own leisure. "Being able to sneak out barefoot with the morning coffee to a spot in the shade, open a newspaper, then get up again for a cold glass of orange juice from inside the house – this must be quality of life in its purest form and made us long for something else," says Van Dinther. "We enjoyed ourselves very much in our apartment in Malmö, in southern Sweden, but we were restless and climbing the walls. We didn't even have a balcony and the idea of 'going down to the park', it's never as easy as it sounds."

Van Dinther is a design writer and art director with clients including *Residence*, among others. He is also *Wallpaper** magazine's eyes and ears in Scandinavia, and in the past few years he has spent over 200 days travelling, both for work and for pleasure. It's something that comes naturally to him after he moved some 30 times around the world during his childhood, along with his three siblings and Dutch parents. Sixteen years ago, when he was living in Stockholm, he met a kindred spirit in copywriter and marketing strategist Wittbjer, who is from Skåne, the southernmost county of Sweden. And although they are very different in many ways, the couple both have a strong interest in design and furnishings.

When the two aesthetes were looking for new accommodation, they searched for something unique, preferably in a muted, elegant style. Numerous showings and a handful of bids later, they found their dream home in a grey stone house from 1842 in the Skåne village of Hunnestad, just over half an hour from Malmö. The house is nestled between soft hills and beautiful fields in the rolling countryside. A few kilometres south lies the sea, and a mere 10-minute walk away is the stately Marsvinsholm Castle, to which the house and its surrounding farm may have previously belonged. Today, the residence consists of two large storage rooms, two bedrooms, a generous bathroom, a large living room that opens into the kitchen and dining room as well as a loft with a combined office and library. In the living room, the high ceiling creates an almost church-like feel that Van Dinther and Wittbjer have softened with a big kelim rug, Ligne Roset's iconic Togo sofa, large auction-purchased urns with green plants and a vintage display table in brass from Italy. In the middle of the room there is a moulded concrete staircase, which appears sculptural with its straight corners and steady expression.

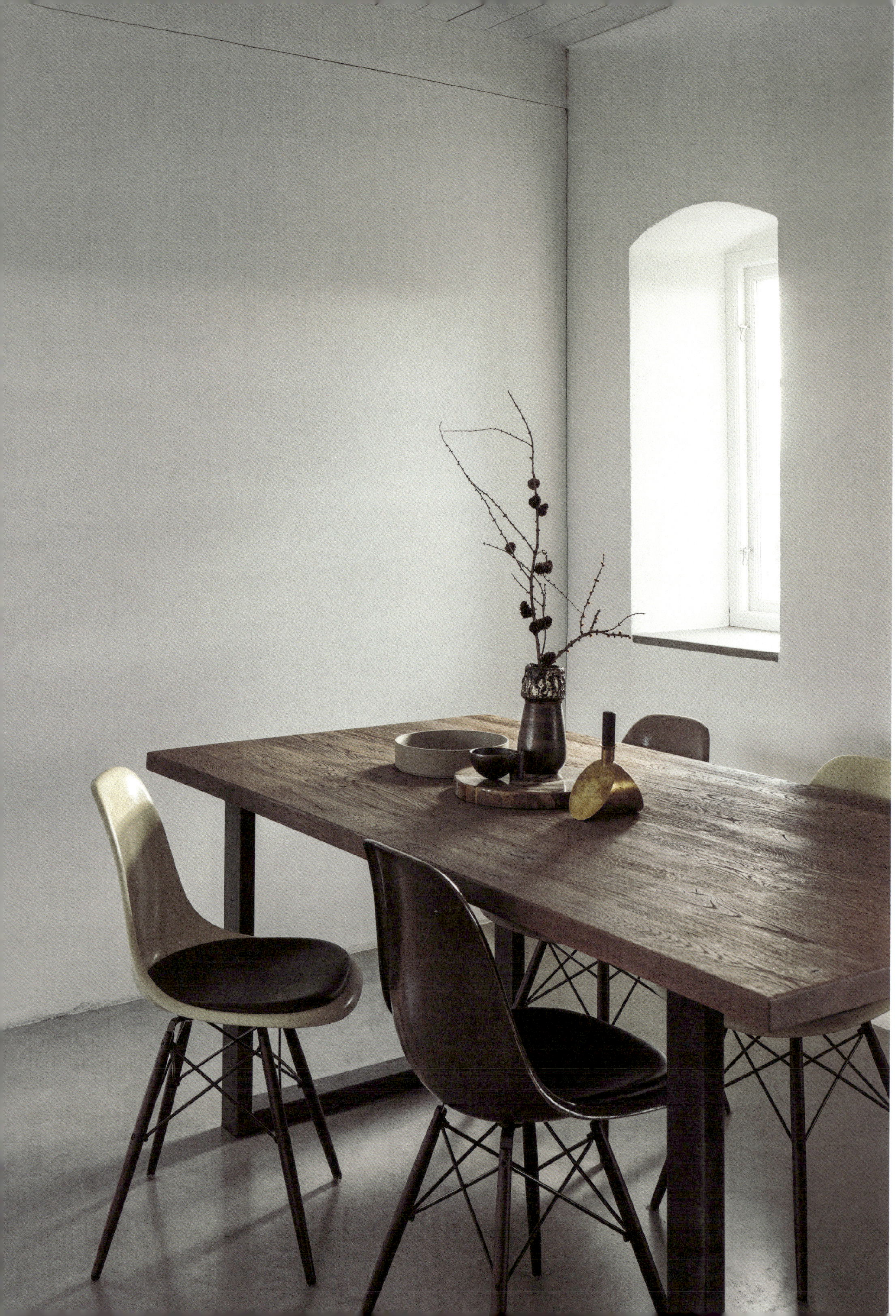

The walls in the house are far from straight and parallel. When the bedroom closet was being built it was necessary to measure every five centimetres. To the left: The larger part of the house is made up of the kitchen and the adjoining sitting room, where the dining table is situated.

Van Dinther is a collector of ceramics that Wittbjer describes as "brown and ragged." To the right: Just outside of the guestroom stands an antique, rustic-style chair and table from the couple's shop, TypeO.

The couple say that the tranquillity and beautiful landscape are the best elements of their new lifestyle, but they still get to experience city life as they spend three days a week working in Malmö. A year ago they decided to share their appreciation of high quality interiors, opening the online shop TypeO, which sells well-chosen design objects. The idea is to offer customers great design products that are not available in most interiors stores. They source new products on their travels, although they are currently enjoying staying at home more often than before, welcoming their foreign friends to Skåne instead. And it is not uncommon for these holiday guests, as they walk out into the beautiful garden, to suddenly decide to move out into the countryside too – seeing the quality of life Van Dinther and Wittbjer dreamed about, and which they have truly managed to create in their house in Hunnestad.

By Michelle Meadows

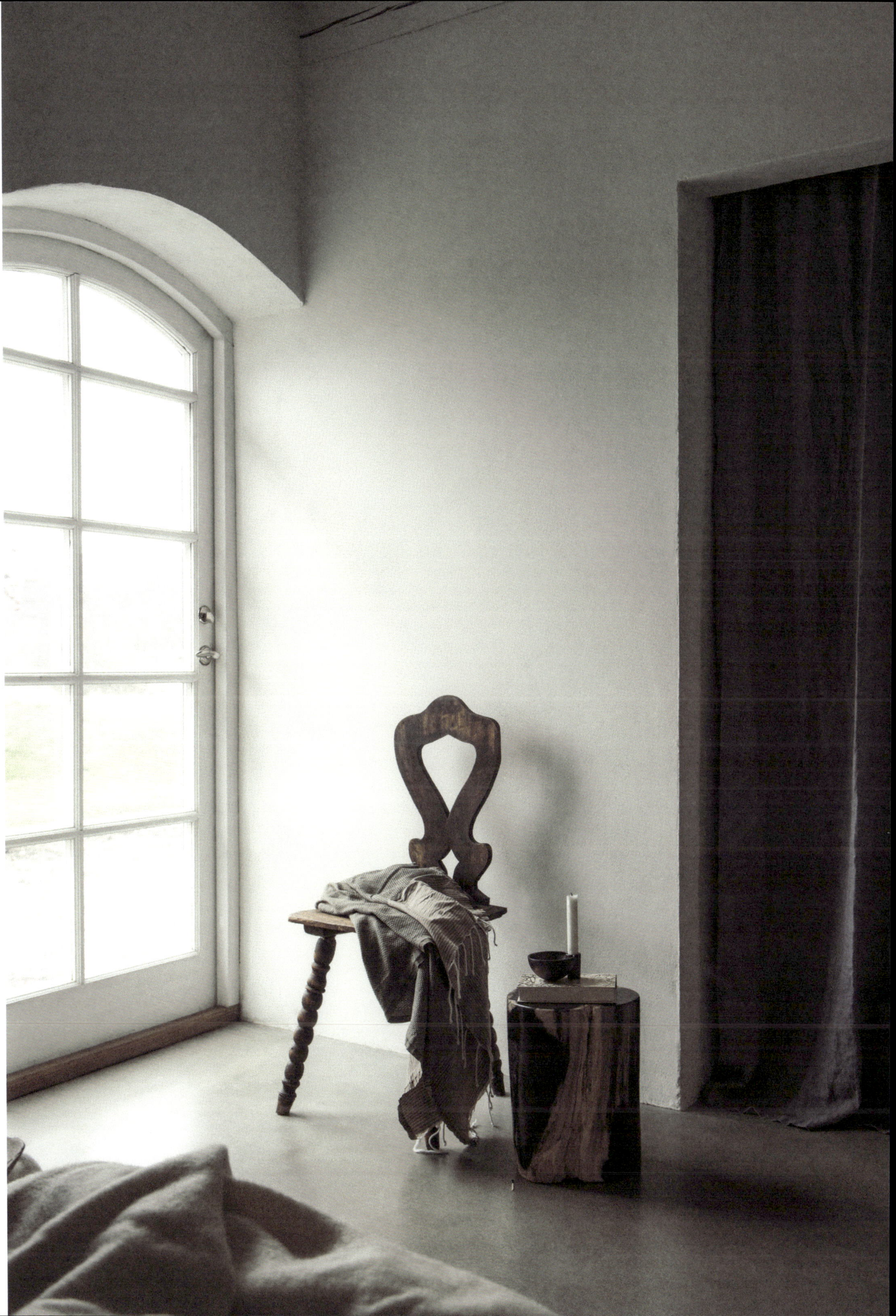

Linn Eklund, 22, belongs to the fourth generation of the family that runs internationally renowned Swedish flooring and textiles company Bolon, founded in 1949 by Nils-Erik Eklund. When she is not helping out with the family business, she studies and works in fashion, including a position as blogger for Swedish Elle – where she has made a name for herself with her strong style and daring combinations.

A colourful persona
LINN EKLUND

THOSE WHO HAVE met Linn Eklund, or just caught a glimpse of her in fashion week snapshots, would probably not raise an eyebrow on walking through the door to the 22-year-old fashionista's flat. Vivid, colourful and vibrating with energy, it perfectly matches the fashion blogger's personality as well as her vibrant clothing experiments.

Eklund's personal style and self-expression came naturally to her during her childhood – she belongs to the fourth generation of the Eklund family, owners of the renowned Bolon flooring and textiles company. The firm was founded in 1949 by Nils-Erik Eklund, and today it is run by Linn Eklund's mother and aunt.

"Of course it has influenced me a great deal to grow up in a design company," says Eklund. "My mother Annica and her sister Marie are my biggest sources of inspiration, and my grandmother is my best friend. My mother has always let me do as I wish and has never tried to push me in any direction. Rather she has encouraged me to find my own style, and when I first moved away from home and became independent, my interest in interior design began to blossom. I began to give shape to my own surroundings, and I realised that I have subconsciously picked up things during my upbringing."

Eklund went to Paris at the age of 19 to study fashion, where her interest in personal style developed. She also spent six months in Hawaii, along with more work-related travel than the busiest of calendars should allow. When she is not helping out with the family business, she is busy studying marketing communications and works as a blogger and fashion writer for *Elle* magazine. She also manages to squeeze in some work for the Stella McCartney store in Stockholm. As a frequent traveller and member of such a vibrant family, Eklund has realised that her style may not always fit into the idea of understated Scandinavian minimalism. "As a person I'm curious, always happy and consider myself to have a colourful personality," she says. "Sweden can actually feel a bit boring to me, beautiful and all, but a bit too minimalist for my taste."

Indeed, spartan is not the word to describe Eklund's current Stockholm home. The apartment is soft and sensuous yet full and sparkling. Patterns, colours and shapes fight for attention. In the centre of the living room, an armchair is covered with graffiti containing a recipe for mashed potatoes. "I've probably redone the apartment 17 times since I moved in," she says. "I have come to realise that it's impossible to cram in all the styles I like in the same flat. At first it was minimalistic and white, with classic furniture like a Gervasoni sofa and a Barcelona chair. I didn't dare to go all out as I was afraid to make mistakes, but after a while I realised it was boring. I painted it dark grey without being aware that it was trendy. I painted the kitchen after being out a bit too late one night during fashion week in Stockholm. The next day I had to go home after a show and happened to pass a paint shop on the way. I walked in, pointed to a colour, went home and painted. Now it's my favourite place in the apartment."

Eklund's passion for interior design is as strong as her interest in fashion, and her approach to creating an inspiring apartment is the same as for composing a perfect outfit. "For me, the two industries go hand in hand, regardless of colours, shapes or patterns," she says. "I never use any guidelines or concepts in advance, I simply pick up things I think are nice, without much thought about how it all goes together. It usually turns out pretty good anyway."

By Tom Cehlin Magnusson

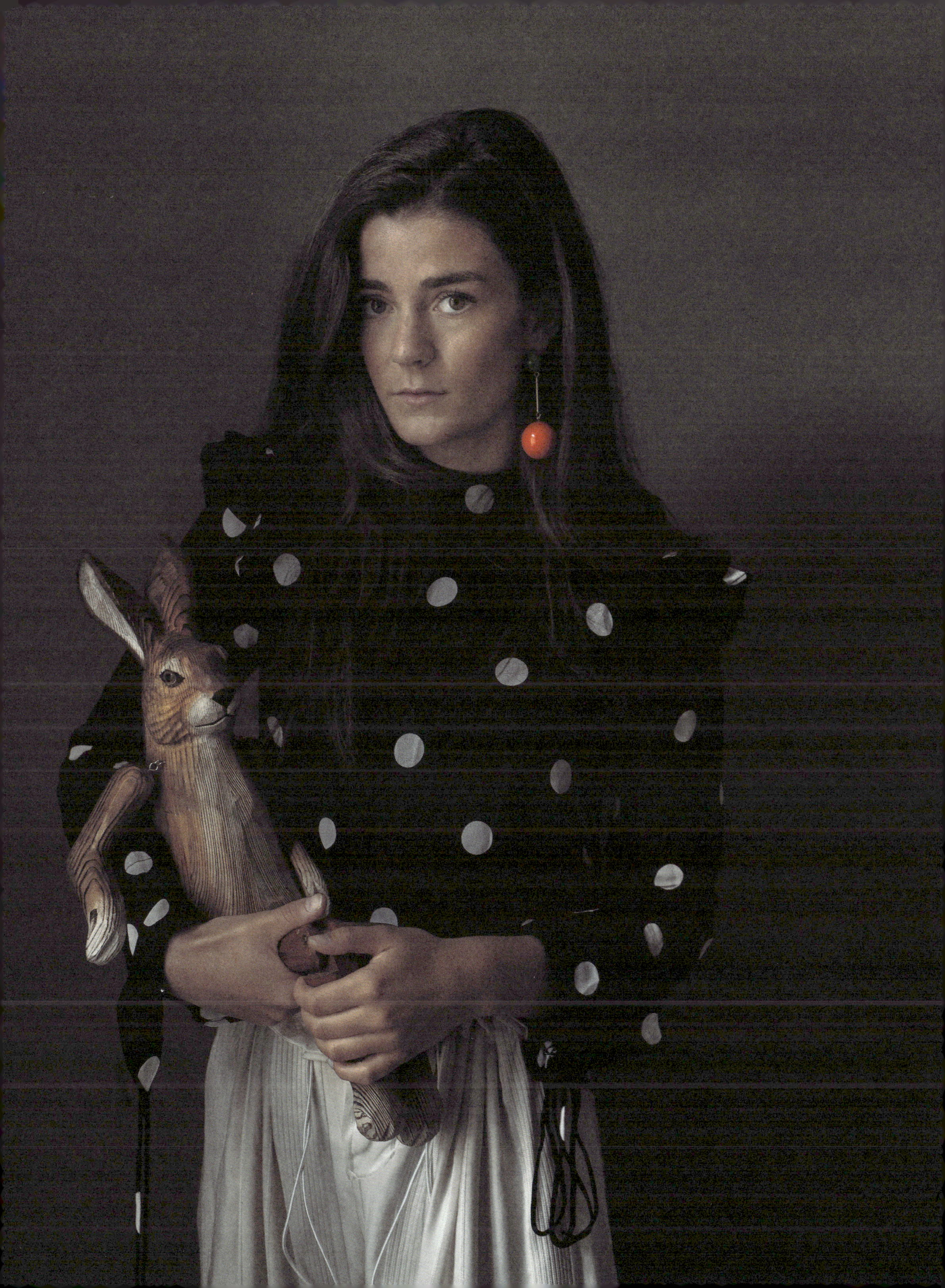

The dramatic colours and patterns in Eklund's apartment are an extension of her personality – if something feels nondescript she repaints without thinking twice. The canopy bed is from Artilleriet. To the right: A custom-designed table by the family's carpenter in Ulricehamn. The lamp is by Gino Sarfatti for Flos and the chairs are by Verner Panton.

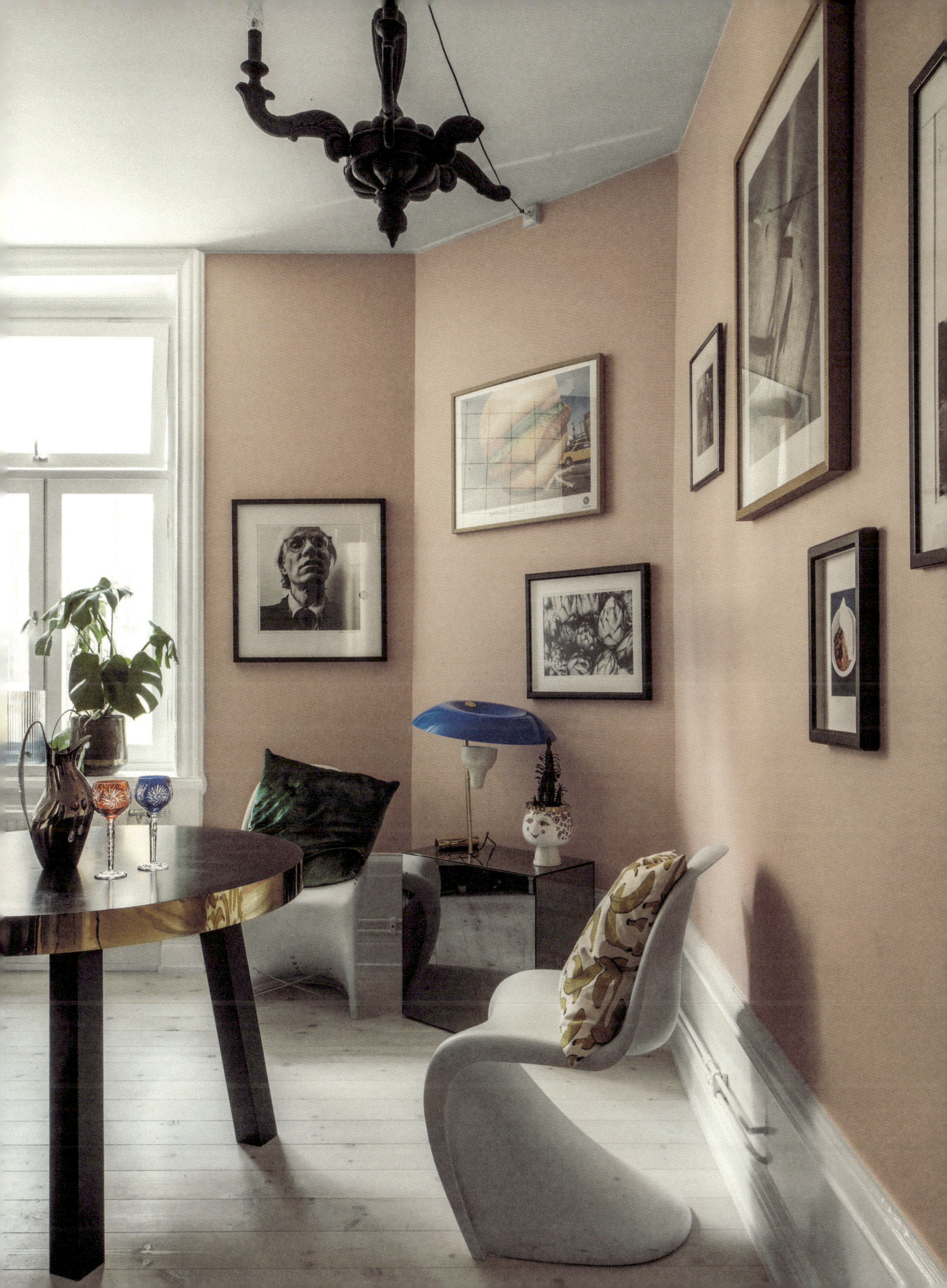

In Linn's airy flat there are traces from the time she spent in Paris as well as her travels to Tokyo. The inhabitants of both cities inspire her when it comes to clothes and interior design. The pink pot is vintage and to the right is a rug from Layered.

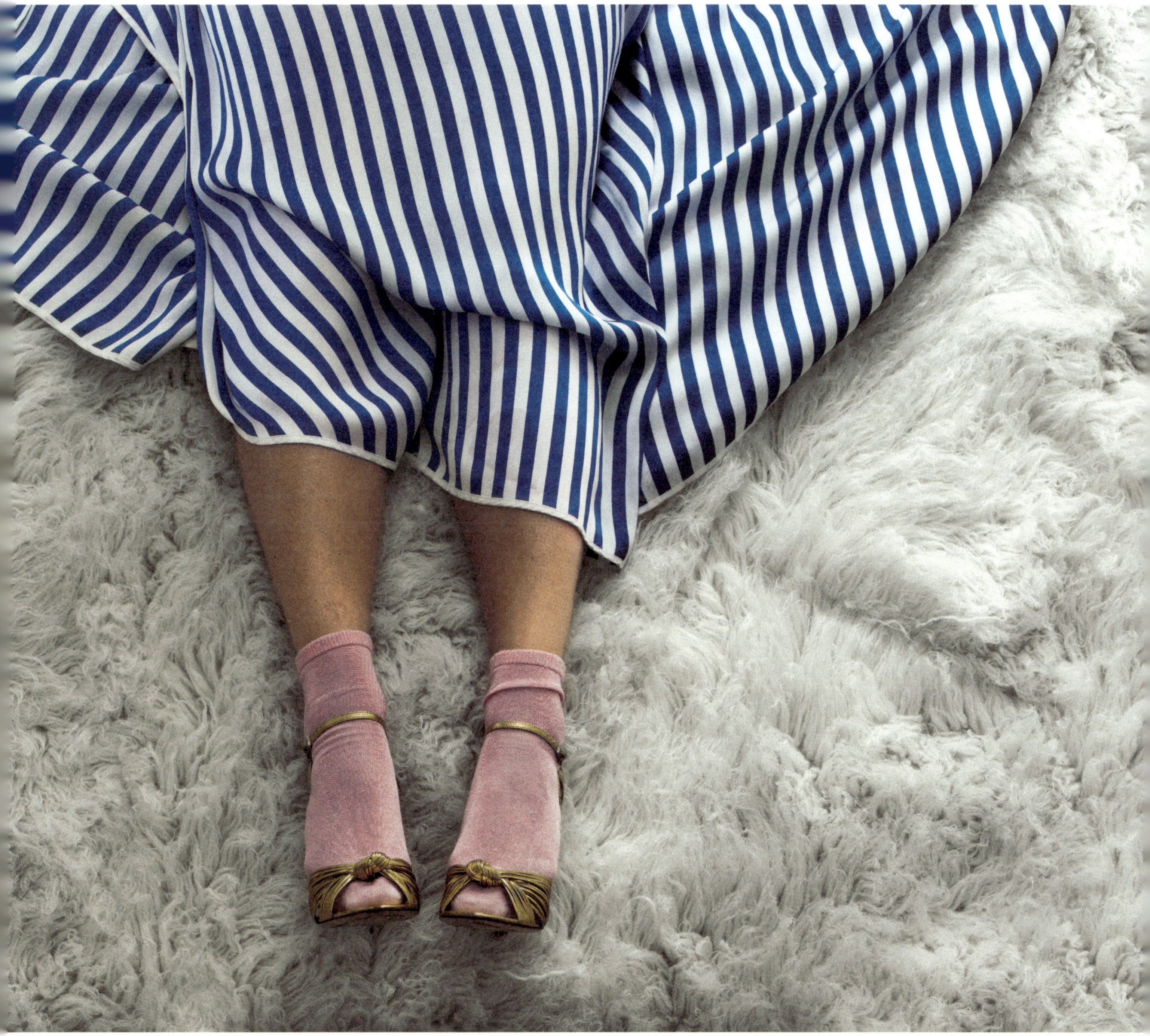

BASED ON A FEELING

"When interior design works well, it allows us to be the best of ourselves."
Hugo Macdonald on the unique appeal of Scandinavian interiors.

THERE WAS A PERIOD last winter when I thought I was going to be hygge-ed to death. What had started in autumn in the UK as an interesting cultural conversation around the Danish concept of hygge had become a marketing juggernaut. In every bookshop there was a dedicated display of new titles telling us how to bring hygge into our lives. Supermarkets, clothing and beauty brands cottoned onto it and rolled it out on everything from winter hampers to socks to bath oils. Bars stocked up on candles and blankets, and renamed happy hour as hygge hour.

By Christmas, you could not open a newspaper or turn on the radio without someone trying first to pronounce hygge, and then explain what it meant. Very quickly the poor word, which had sat quietly untouched in Danish culture for centuries, was everywhere, consigned to the realm of commercial kitsch, nothing more than an excuse for a cupcake or a mug of glogg. This winter, marketing departments have headed north to Sweden and decided that lagom – meaning 'just the right amount' – is what we all need. At least it is easier to pronounce.

The issue here, as is so often the case when cultural nuances get hijacked for commercial gain, is that there is little consideration given to the complexity of context. Hygge is something far more than cake, closed curtains and candlelight. Lagom is more than a small plate of cured salmon and rye bread. They are subtle ways of living that require a form of communion and unspoken consensus, and hence they belong in the cultures in which they exist. They can't easily be transplanted or taught, and definitely not bought.

The same can be said for the Scandinavian interior. In the last issue of *My Residence*, I wrote a piece about what we – outside

Scandinavia – can learn about interior life from our friends in the north. My conclusion was fairly straightforward: that the Scandinavian interior is a feeling, more than an aesthetic, and that elsewhere we have confused this delicate balance, believing that copying the look means we can achieve the feeling. I have carried this thought in my head over the past year in an attempt to better understand where that feeling comes from.

It is made up of many elements that come together to be something greater than the sum of their parts: materials, light, patina and colour, for instance. After many more visits to various places in the Nordic region, it strikes me that there is one common element at the foundation of the Scandinavian interior, which doesn't get so much recognition because it is harder to articulate. It is an innate acknowledgement of people and human behaviour. It is an understanding of needs and feelings, and an anticipated response to these is embedded in the design approach, from architecture to interiors, furniture, lighting and even smaller objects. The best term to describe this intangible quality is hospitality.

By hospitality I don't mean a literal meeting of host and guest in a hotel or a home. It's a deeper, subtler recognition of the importance that design can play in comfortably bringing us together. In the domestic interior it starts with understanding one's sense of self, in having the confidence to create an environment that is a comfortable expression and extension of one's being. A personal environment allows people to feel happy to be themselves. And when someone is comfortable in their own interior world and in their own skin, they are open to letting others in.

The Scandinavian interior is an important part of how Scandinavian people communicate themselves to others, and I believe a compelling part of this communication is based not on the aesthetic, but in something more implicit. It is not the design of the space itself, it is the effect that the design has on us, how it makes us feel and behave, that enables us to come together easily and naturally. This is an embedded sense of hospitality in design.

In spring, I visited a series of homes on a route from Stockholm down through southern Sweden to Malmo. To compare them by design alone would not reveal much similarity beyond the occasional Design House Stockholm candlestick. What they shared could not be communicated in pictures. They were each an unequivocal expression of their owners' lives and personalities. Consequently, they felt entirely inhabited and comfortable. Thought had clearly gone into how each home worked to support the life of its resident, from the layout and furnishing to the last detail of how things were stored or objects arranged for ease and pleasure of use. This was real life, not styling.

You might assume that in creating a personal environment, it could be confrontational to then invite a relative stranger into that world. But in fact the opposite is true. Such was the comfort of each inhabitant in each home that the notion of hospitality was natural. There was nothing awkward, forced or precious in the experiences of staying in these homes. It was easy and effortless. When an interior has been designed with a conscious understanding of how it supports the wants and needs of the people who move through it, then it is a joy to inhabit, whether as owner or guest. A sense of hospitality does not require the owner of a home to be present. Using Airbnb in Scandinavia is a good way of experiencing how thoughtful interior design can make guests feel at home, even in the absence of a host. I have stayed in a few apartments in Copenhagen and Stockholm that, even after just two nights, have been extremely difficult to leave, such was their ease of inhabitation.

Why is this notion of hospitality so strong in the Scandinavian interior? A lazy answer might point to the long winters, which is the easy response to so many social and cultural idiosyncrasies of the region. Long, dark winters have perhaps instilled a need for a more developed understanding of how to create interiors that allow for people to spend long periods of time indoors without going mad, alone or in company. But there's definitely more to it than this. There is no doubt that having a closer relationship to nature and the natural environment plays an important part. The Scandinavian interior goes further than a skilled use of natural materials and natural light in design, acknowledging and understanding the importance of natural inhabitation too.

I believe that the answer also lies in a layer of Scandinavian social culture, particular to different countries and regions, that acknowledges how people behave, individually and together. Words such as lagom and hygge are just two examples of this, expressing the intricate relationship between self and others, nature and space, activity and atmosphere. They reveal an understanding of how all these elements of life are inextricably linked and suggest that there is a positive order – a rhythm – that comes with practising them. In my understanding, it is paying attention to this layer of living and being that makes Scandinavian interiors so inhabitable, and hospitable.

When interior design works well, it allows us to be the best of ourselves. It removes the need for us to work at making sense of our surroundings and frees us up to be present. It is implicit, not explicit, and embedded, rather than surface, in its application. This is a common thread that connects much of the design philosophy across Scandinavia, from the pioneers of post-war modernism through to the vanguards of contemporary design today. It is an understanding that design is not something to get in the way, not something to be noticed, but rather something to enable and facilitate us in our daily lives. It acknowledges that our interiors play a crucial role in our physical and emotional wellbeing, recognising that they should be inhabitable environments, but also hospitable, to ourselves and others. The reason why we find Scandinavian interior life so compelling is because it makes everyone feel welcome.

Hugo Macdonald is a design consultant living between London and Hastings. He was formerly the brand director of Studioilse, Ilse Crawford's design studio, and design editor of Monocle magazine. His first book, How to Live in the City, was published in 2016 by Pan Macmillan for the School of Life.

CELEBRATING THE BEST OF SWEDISH DESIGN

Every year Residence celebrates Sweden's most notable designs with its annual prize. Here we present some of this year's winners.

Launch of the year
ARKET

H&M's new brand Arket is about timeless elegance, classic cuts and durable items, both in clothing and interior design accessories. Swedish classics are interspersed with a specially produced series by Swedish designers such as Carina Seth Andersson. When architect and interior designer Christian Halleröd collaborated with Arket on the chain's café, he chose a chair design by Swedish master Carl Malmsten. The original model was designed in the 1930s, when rustic, sturdy lodge furniture was popular. Original drawings were missing, so the new chairs for Arket were manufactured by Tre Sekel based on copies sold at auction.

Lighting of the year
W171 ALMA LAMP

The W171 Alma lamp – originally designed for the beautiful Alma members' club in Stockholm – spreads light like ripples on water. The minimalist disk hangs beautifully on the ceiling, suspended over the dining table or even as an artwork on the wall. The lamp was designed by architects Tham & Videgård and is produced by Wästberg.

Producer of the year
DUX

The Swedish furniture brand Dux was founded in 1926, and since then it has been adorning Swedish homes with classics by designers such as Bruno Mathsson, among others. Since the next generation of the family has taken over the company, it has entered into a new phase and made a solid investment in contemporary Swedish design, with an ambitious collection by architects Claesson Koivisto Rune. The Arizona, Dakota, Montana and Ohio tables are like smart steel sketches, and the collection also features generous sofa systems, the exquisite Anita armchair and various cabinets.

Accessory of the year
124 BY DANIEL RYBAKKEN FOR ARTEK

124 degrees of everyday magic – Daniel Rybakken's 124 mirror for Artek opens out like a book at an angle of 124 degrees, turning the room into a mirrored world of unexpected angles and highlights.

Designer of the year
CHRIS MARTIN

Last year Massproductions was producer of the year, and this year the company's chief designer, Chris Martin, has been awarded designer of the year. Martin's elegant furniture has a look that manages to be both contemporary and timeless. His Spark Lounge Chair, which balances ease, strength and surprising comfort, was inspired by the Nordic kicksled, and is also reminiscent of early aircraft.

Furniture item of the year
BLECK SOFA

The Bleck sofa, designed by TAF Architects for Gärsnäs, took inspiration from the aesthetics of a tension frame. Bleck sits well in the middle of a room, to showcase the interesting features of the back of the sofa, with its notable combination of materials and carpentry.

Craftsmanship of the year
K.F.K. SNICKERI

The award of craftsmanship this year goes to the young master cabinet makers K.F.K. Snickeri, for the beautiful furniture they have created on behalf of interior designers, shops and a growing number of private custumers. Their collaboration with interior designer Louise Liljencrantz, Liljencrantz x K.F.K., has resulted in the fantastic Seed series, which includes the table pictured.

Interior designer of the year
LOUISE LILJENCRANTZ

The award of interior designer of the year goes to Louise Liljencrantz for all the elegant environments and homes she has created for both property developers and private customers. As well as creating beautiful interiors, she also designs her own furniture. The Pin Coat Rack was created by Liljencrantz for a client and is now available to order.

Joanna Hummel is head of Swedish hair and beauty franchise Lyko. Daniel Hummel works in banking and real estate. They live with their four children in a suburban house outside Stockholm, and during holidays they decamp to the Bungenäs peninsula, which juts out from Gotland, the most popular of the Swedish islands. Here they have built their maintenance-free dream house, paving the way for simple and pleasurable vacations.

Only the necessities
JOANNA & DANIEL HUMMEL

JOANNA AND DANIEL HUMMEL are the sort of people who get things done. While some of us dream away the day sketching castles in the air, the Hummels make things happen. They both have experience of holding executive positions and have clear visions about what they do and don't want. So when, at the age of 41, Joanna decided she had endured enough holidays at other people's country abodes and needed a place to call their own where they could entertain their four children during the summer, things took off quickly.

Daniel called his friend, entrepreneur Joachim Kuylenstierna, who back in 2007 purchased 160 hectares of land on Bungenäs, a peninsula in the northern part of Gotland – the island on which a large part of the Swedish population has spent at least one summer. The area was formerly used as a military training base, after the limestone quarry here was deserted in the 1960s. Bungenäs offers a mixture of abandoned industrial land and old trenches and bunkers where nature has taken over to create a breathtaking, unique landscape. The area has now become a tourist destination, home to a series of striking contemporary architectural projects.

Within two weeks the Hummels had purchased a plot and began designing a house with Joel Phersson from architecture firm Skälsö, which had initially designed the zoning plan for the entire area. The plot is on a hill, with two levels – one lower, with the sun from the south in the sparse pine forest, and another situated higher up to give views of the dramatic quarry, the Baltic sea in the west and the evening sun. The challenge was how to make the most of both of these aspects – and to integrate the house without losing the unique qualities of the landscape. "We wanted to have a kitchen with close proximity to the garden, several bedrooms on the same level, no thresholds, and a pool that can be seen easily from the house and two bathrooms," says Daniel.

These requests were solved by Skälsö, with a house that climbs up the hill on two levels. "The upper level with the social rooms is open to the quarry as well as to the sea," says Phersson. "Here the glass walls are large and operable, a seamless transition to the large cement deck outside with a dining table, pool and sunning area. The lower level is private. The building ends here yet simultaneously creates a protected garden where the sun warms up the area even on windy days."

The pool was discussed extensively, not least because it took up a large chunk of the budget. "The pool has made our lives so much

PHOTOGRAPHY: LINA EIDENBERG ADAMO

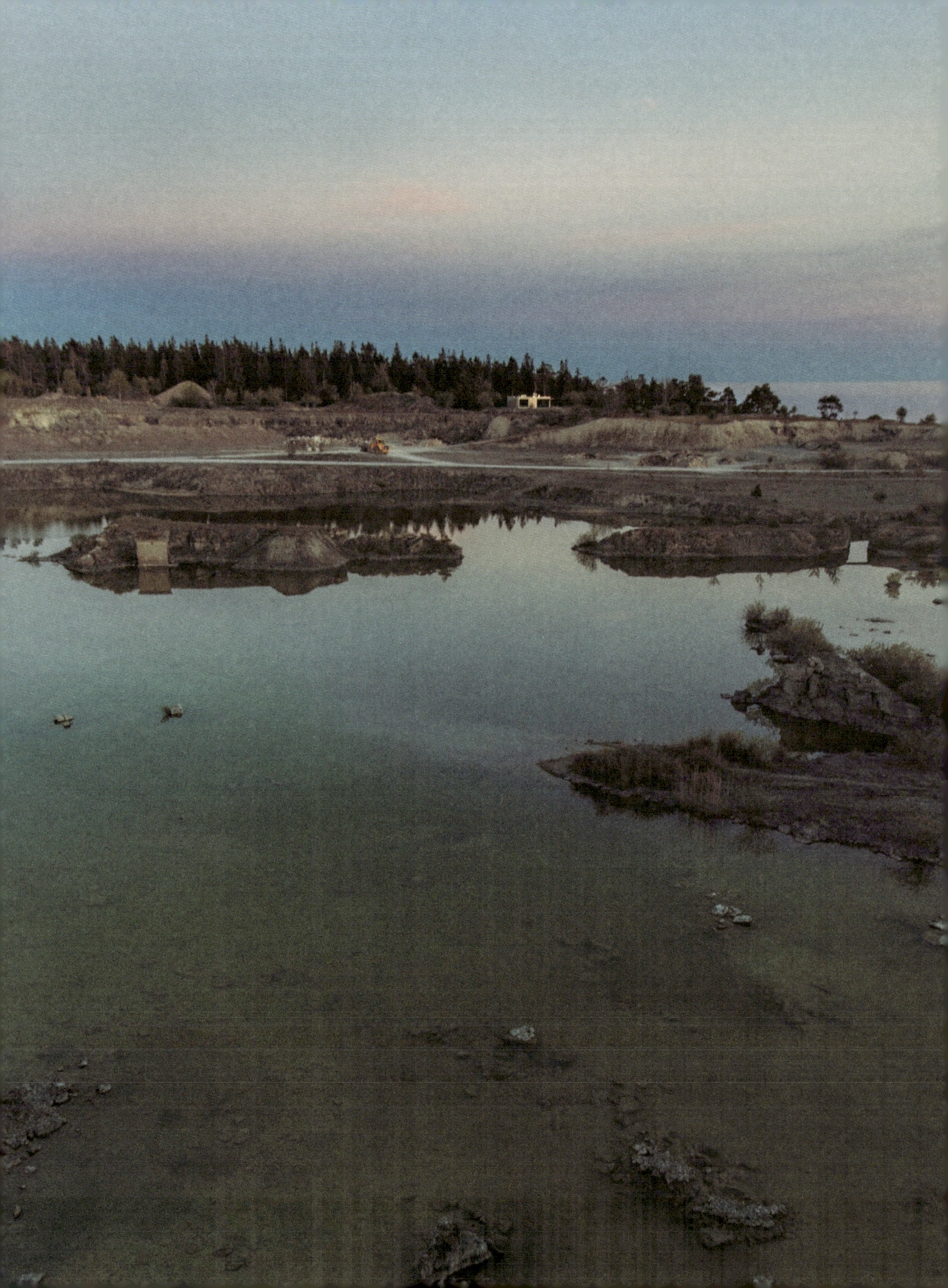

*The colour of the water in the nearby limestone quarry is reflected in the family's cast cement pool.
The chairs are by Fermob and the On-The-Move table is from Cane-line.*

A common theme throughout the construction of the house was that it should work side by side with the geography and surrounding nature. The clean and simple lines allow the materials to speak for themselves, and life between outside and inside is as seamless as one could wish of a summerhouse.

easier," says Joanna. "When you have four children and everyone has to be given breakfast, poolside is the perfect place to have your own sandwich when the kids are finished with theirs. Because they are itching to get going right after breakfast, they can jump into the pool on our own property and we can then get a chance to read the morning paper."

After the first summer in the house, the family became so taken with the maintenance-free lifestyle that they now want to sell their main house in a Stockholm suburb and move to a more easily maintained flat in the city. "I have come to realise that too many possessions and too much space can be overwhelming," says Joanna. "In our summer cottage we have only the things we need. We haven't taken a single old item there and decorated entirely from scratch. Every dish we have is necessary."

Life is a bit different in Bungenäs. Cars must be left at the entrance to the area, so visitors explore the unusual surroundings by bike or by foot, which the family has fully embraced. "The first year I was outside Bungenäs only twice," says Joanna. "It dawned on me that I started to wonder which was the real world – the one inside the limestone quarry or the one outside it. We go to the house any time of year, autumn as well as spring. In the summer it is truly a paradise for the children, who bike to friends, buy ice cream on our account at the kiosk and build play huts in the abandoned quarry."

By Imke Janoschek

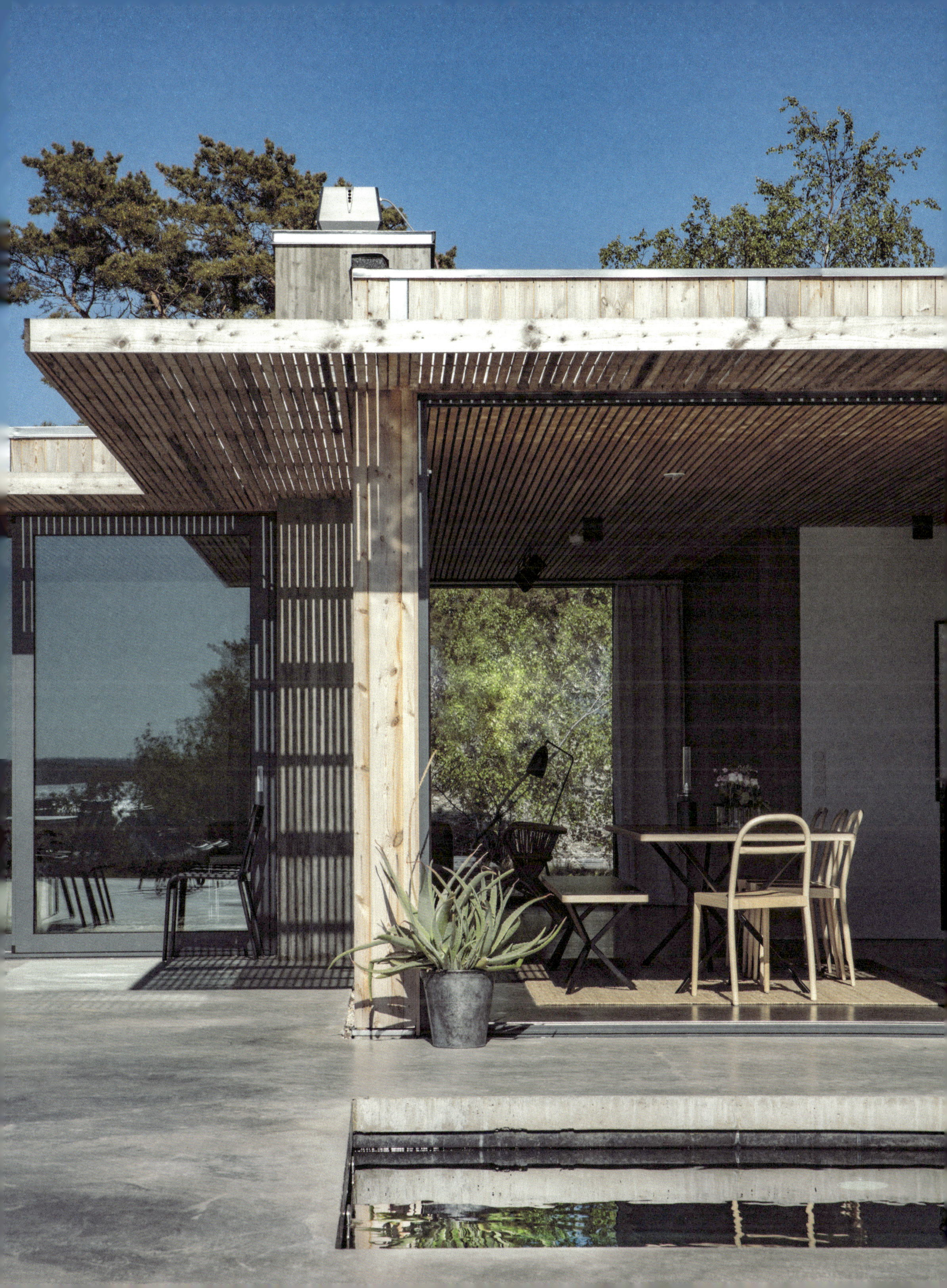

Frama was founded by Niels Strøyer Christophersen five years ago. The company's studio store in Copenhagen is located in a former pharmacy dating back to 1878. Frama's Sintra marble table comes in various combinations and sizes, and the daybed is a prototype launching in 2018.

TRIBE FRAMA

Niels Strøyer Christophersen on the importance of spaces, good collaborations and building a culturally orientated furniture brand.

SINCE 2013, Danish design brand Frama has operated from its headquarters in a former Copenhagen pharmacy, St Pauls Apotek, dating back to 1878. As a furniture producer, Frama sets its own agenda, not limiting itself to only producing furniture and focusing on traditional trade fairs, but also finding new ways to collaborate with likeminded people in similar fields, ranging from food to art. As well as launching Frama Studio Stores in Oslo and Stockholm, the firm has also started up an artist residency programme in Italy.

"Frama started out as a trading agency and eventually we shifted to making our own products," says founder Niels Strøyer Christophersen. "We always strived to have a certain balance in the collection, where commercially orientated pieces meet more bespoke pieces. It's a matter of maintaining integrity and not going for quick fixes."

How would you describe the culture you have built inside and around Frama?

"My hope is that when you are communicating with Frama in one way or another, you feel that the company has a certain character. The company is built on a cultural lifestyle, and this absolutely generates a kind of tribe culture inside and around Frama. Working with people who appreciate similar values, and also feel a responsibility for the society we live in, makes our company much more holistic. It also makes business a little less rigid and corporate, even though you can't avoid certain frameworks. We often host different events in collaboration with brands that share the same mindset, and it's always a very nice, casual experience. I like Frama to be a company with healthy values – this is high up on our agenda. It's something that needs to be constantly maintained while growing; it doesn't come without effort."

What other companies do you find interesting, and which types of business inspire you?

"I'm inspired by companies that are able to be consistent and maintain integrity. It is also interesting if the company can keep adapting to the future. I find the templates of Porsche and Apple interesting, working around the same chassis for decades. It's not enough to be creative today; you have to have a strong opinion about business and strategies and insure integrity and consistency. Operations and logistics take as much effort as the frontier of the brand.

I think comfort is the biggest challenge for a creatively driven company, and you need a very strong vision in order to maintain continuous development. It is very motivating observing other companies. In Japan they say that observing is the actual design phase."

Frama is only five years old, but has definitely found its tone and audience. What have been the biggest business decisions?

"The most important decision on this journey so far has been the acknowledgement that products are products, and at the end of the day it's the people in touch with these pieces that make them relevant. Creating a team that is 100 per cent dedicated, believes in the brand philosophy and actually takes the company to another level has been of great importance. Another important business decision for us is to not compare ourselves with other companies, because you will only end up being a reflection of something that already exists."

How important are the spaces you create – your home studio, your space at St Pauls and also the studio stores?

"Spaces are important to us because they place our pieces from

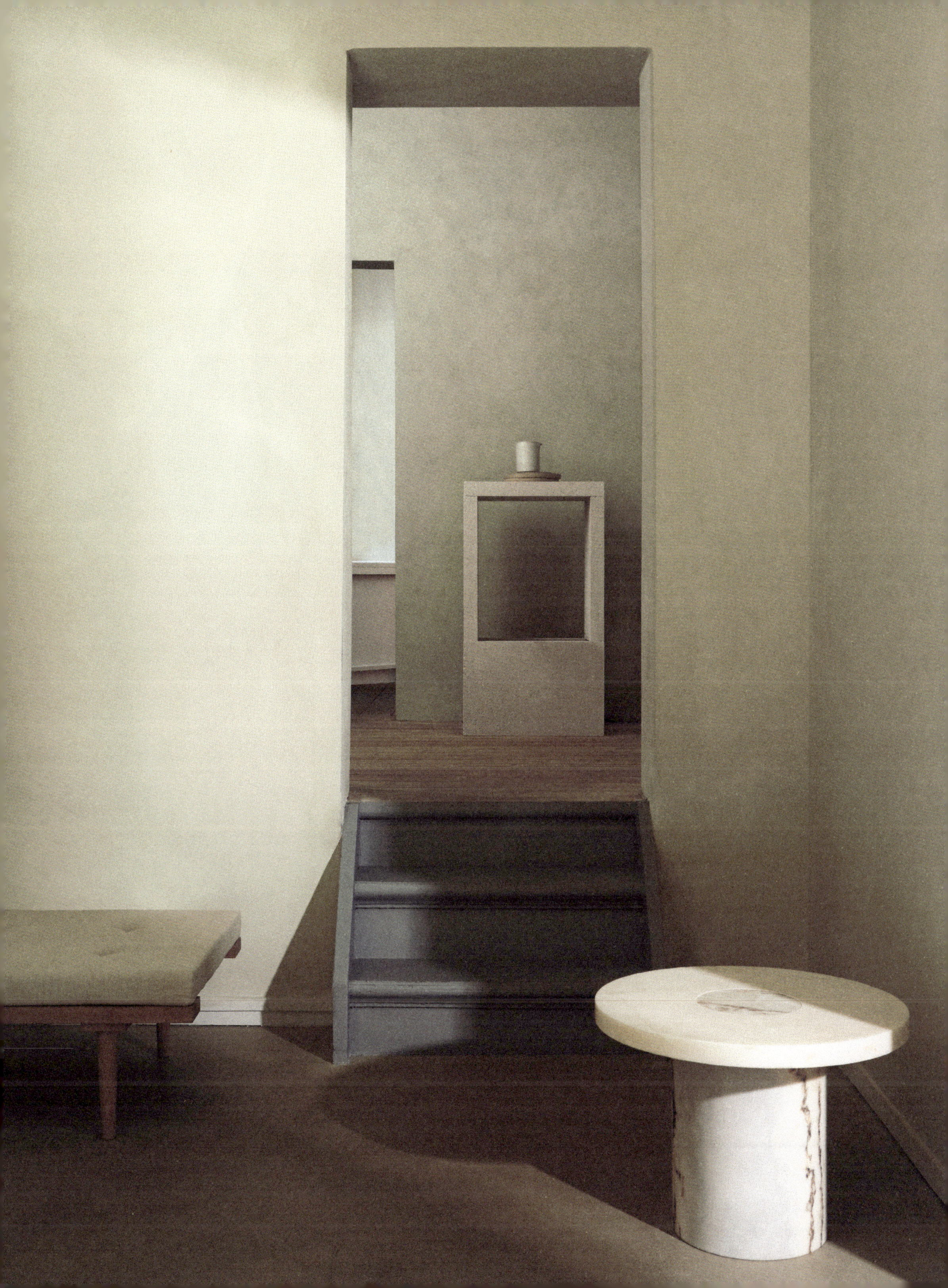

PHOTOGRAPHY: MICHAEL RYGAARD

Niels Strøyer Christophersen in the Frama Studio Apartment, which is also his home, with vintage chair and Sintra coffee table. To the left: One of the rooms in the Frama Studio Store in Copenhagen. The brass object was handmade by local steel smith Toke Lauridsen. The aim is that the interiors, often changing in colour and expression, should always feel calm and harmonious.

across all the collections in a specific environment. We believe in calm spaces where you are able to feel present and relevant as a person, and where you feel inspired and motivated to be creative. We also believe that spaces should somehow invite healthy dialogue and conversation, and almost act as a refuge from the noise of urban society. Our spaces express honesty and simplicity, and the overall feel is not that the space should feel 'designed', but instead be in natural harmony."

What characteristics do you look for in your collaborators?

"We collaborate with likeminded people, brands and companies where we can see a synergy between the parties. Frama is the result of many collaborations and projects, and this is one of the characteristics of the company; that we believe in sharing ideas and thoughts that can lead to something new and unique. Characteristics such as originality and passion are equally important to us when choosing collaborators. The Frama mentality is very intuitive and straightforward, with a naive approach that 'everything is possible'."

How do you see the role of the furniture producer evolving?

"In most cases it's the marketing departments that dictate what furniture should be introduced. It clearly reflects the business of the furniture industry today, and in most cases the creator behind the product doesn't have much say when it comes to final decisions or how he/she believes it should be introduced. When very commercial powers rule the market, a product rarely survives for long before it's replaced with yet another new thing. As a furniture producer it's not enough to think about sustainable production, you also have to have

The ceramic Aj Otto dinnerware on top of the shelf is handcrafted locally in Denmark. The shapes of the Aj Otto series have a timeless and Scandinavian aesthetic, combined with a stackable function and a delicate glaze. To the right: The Shelf Library System is fastened to the wall of the Copenhagen studio with stainless steel screws on solid oak rails. The shelves can easily be placed and restyled in a variety of ways.

a clear vision about your intentions for the product and its life cycle. It's interesting to see how this business will evolve over the next decade, because the larger players on the established market start suffering from their very aggressive market approaches, and stores can't follow the fast flow of products being introduced. The end consumers are starting to request a slower news cycle. It can easily become a healthy game changer over the coming years."

You have made a book and you are involved in an artist programme called Frama Brescia – two quite unusual projects for a furniture producer to take on.

"Our mentality is very intuitive and straightforward, and when something feels right we act on it, in most cases at least. When we meet and talk to people, new opportunities arise, and this is one of the things that drives the company forward. We never know what is around the corner, and it's an important direction to maintain. Our first book, *Dialogues*, was a major project for us, and we are very proud of the result. It definitely carries a clear Frama stamp, as we call it, and considering the amount of collaborators involved we maintained our integrity. Everybody involved in the creative field knows how difficult it is to insure the original idea and concept last all the way to the market."

Tell us about your involvement in Frama Brescia.

"We like to be a culture-orientated company rather than a product-based company. Frama Brescia is the first 'off the grid' project, where we support artists in partnership with the Scaroni-Monti family at Palazzo Monti. The palazzo is located in the Italian town of

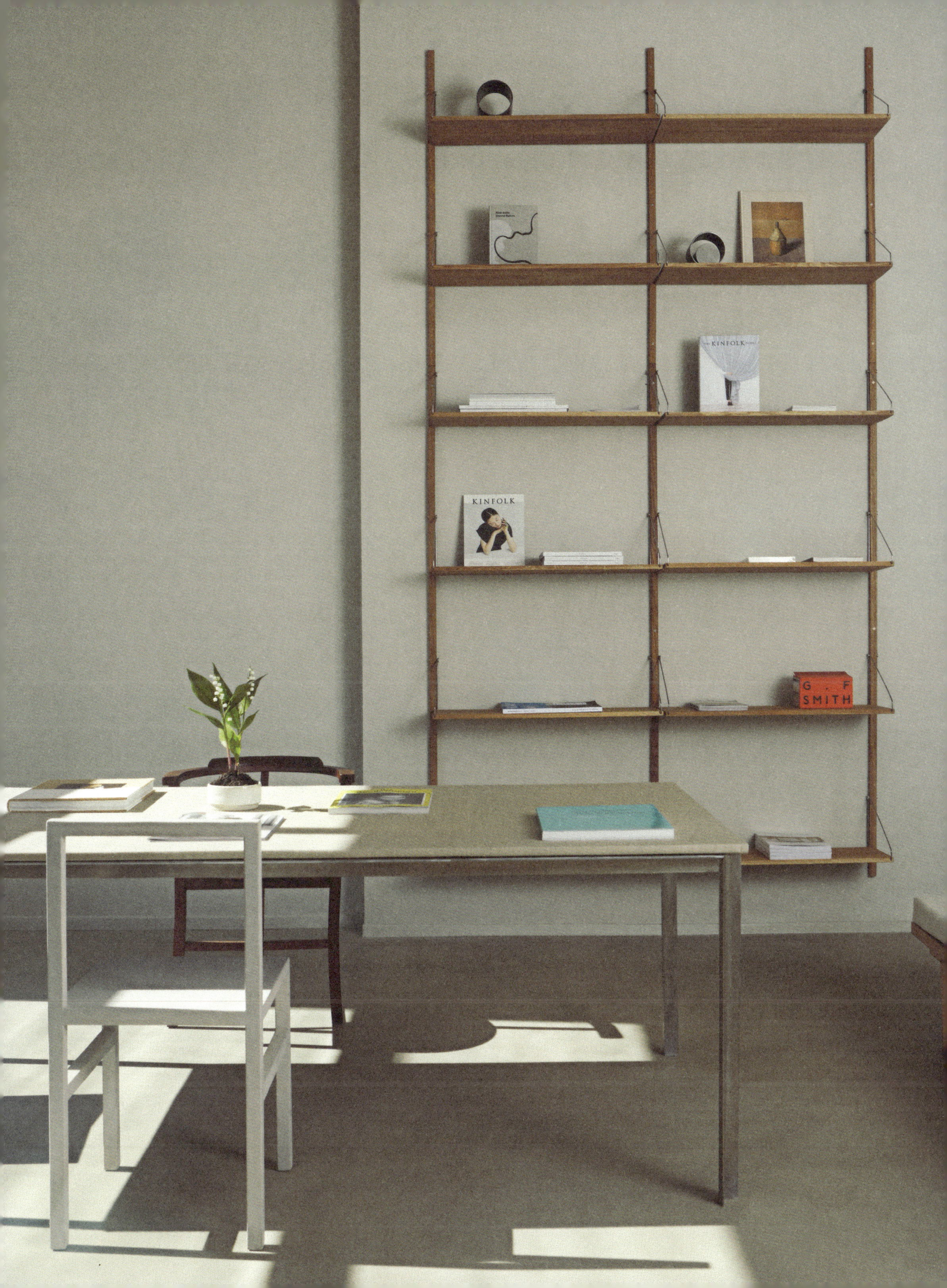
KINFOLK
G . F
SMITH

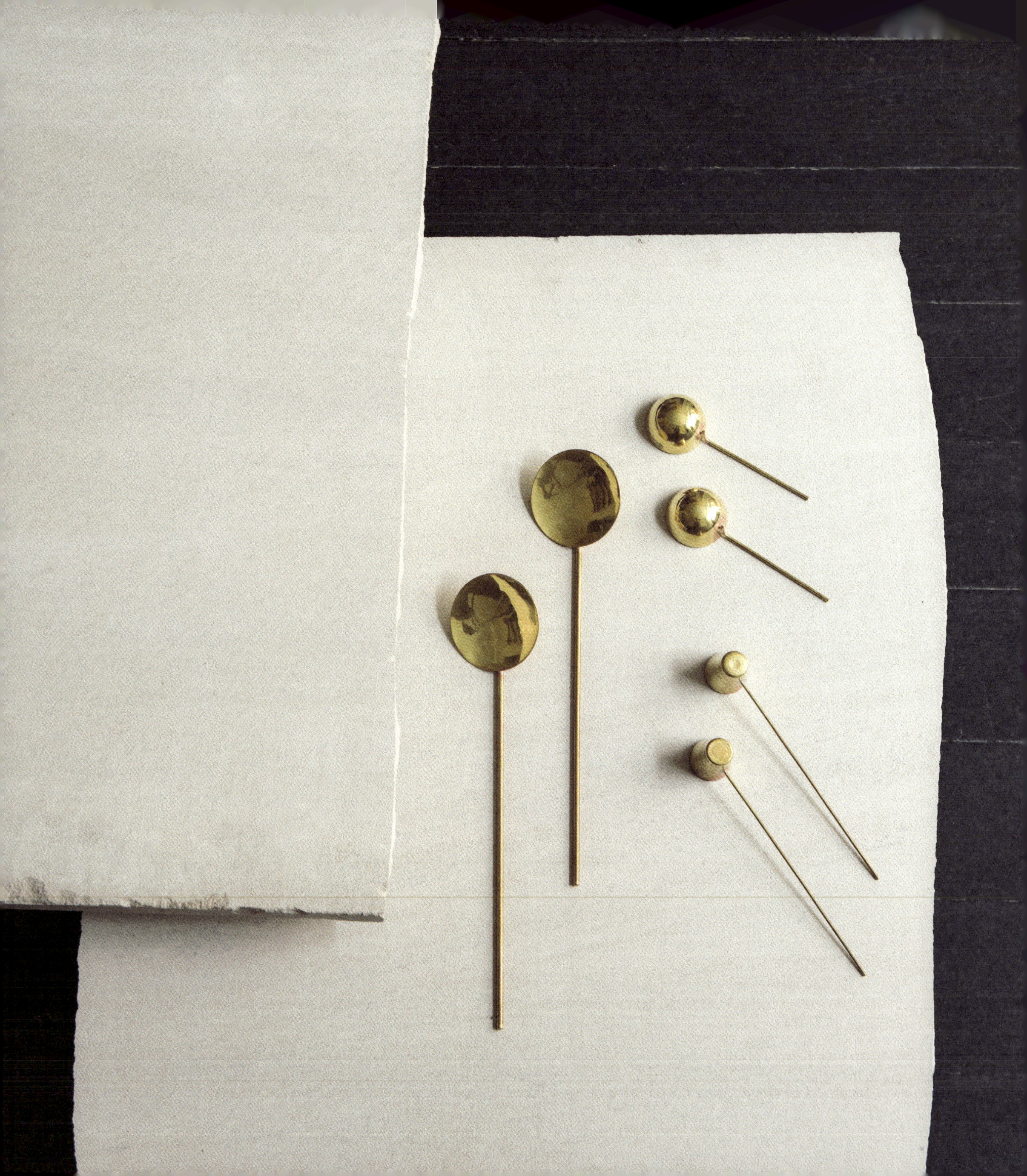

Fredrik Egeland Aartun and Johanne Aurebekk from Frama, outside the newly opened Frama Studio Store in Stockholm, located at Dry Studios in Upplandsgatan. To the left: The handmade brass spoons are by Norwegian design duo Kneip.

PHOTOGRAPHY: LASSE FLØDE

Above is the bedroom at Palazzo Monti, located in the Italian town of Brescia and built in the 13th century. The Danish artist Leonardo Anker Amadeus Vandal was the first artist to check in at Palazzo Monti. He has unveiled over 20 pieces of art and design inspired by northern Italy since he arrived. To the left: The newly opened Kollekted by / Frama Studio Store in Oslo.

Brescia and was built in the 13th century. It's a beautiful space, and the ambition is to give artists and creative talents the possibility to explore their ideas in an interesting setting. So we set up the artist residency – as a project it's meaningful not only to the artists but also to us."

How did your collaborations with Oslo shop Kollekted By and Dry Studios in Stockholm come about? They are not traditional shops within shops, but more based on supporting each other?

"In many cases Frama and Kollekted By have been following similar paths in terms of how our business directions were growing. A few years ago we decided to establish a stronger profile and named our partnership Kollekted By / Frama. We push and support each other, and it's inspiring to see the brand through their eyes. Kollekted By now act as agents for the Norwegian market, and with the new 200-square-metre Kollekted By / Frama store we will be able to showcase the brand universe in a much more dedicated way. The collaboration with Dry in Stockholm is quite new and we now have a Frama Studio Store in their amazing space at Upplandsgatan. We're sure that many interesting collaborations will come out of this friendship; good collaborations go deeper than just exchanging goods."

What is the best advice you have received since you started Frama?

"To listen to yourself, in both your private and professional spheres. At the end of the day, both areas of your life are connected, and if there is an imbalance then it will affect the other part of your life. With all the noise from media, entertainment and communication channels that we are surrounded by today, it is actually quite hard to connect with yourself and maintain this inner communication with your body and mind."

By Hanna Nova Beatrice

Swedish furniture brand Asplund, founded in 1990 and run by Sandra Adrian Asplund and brothers Thomas and Michael Asplund, contributed to putting Swedish design on the map internationally. The business has always focused on working with talented designers, who have helped create bestselling furniture icons such as the Snö and Tati series.

Creating the right flow
SANDRA ADRIAN ASPLUND

SANDRA ADRIAN ASPLUND, creative director of Swedish furniture brand Asplund, sees herself more as a caretaker than a creator. "I take in a lot of information and input from designers, customers and the world at large," she says. "Then I process things over time, and when I least expect it, I suddenly see the products and their value in a larger thematic context. At that moment, I also have the entire course clearly in front of me. I take all the steps in the process into consideration at once, to get a sense of the whole picture and a course to follow in our product development."

When is a product good according to you?

"It has to do with several aspects. Clearly, it should be aesthetically appealing, but at the same time functional and durable. I feel nauseous when I think of all the waste that goes on. However, providing both craftsmanship and sustainability in the products we create at Asplund has proved difficult at times. Most people today are accustomed to how fast everything happens when things are mass-produced. We primarily make furniture upon request only, which means having to wait. People are generally not used to waiting, and then our task becomes getting them to understand that it is worth the wait."

You mean that you try to influence people's consumer behaviour?

"We can do nothing but simply try and maintain our standards. This has been a common theme since the beginning in 1990. Of course, I can see a big difference between now and then. We are obviously extremely interested in the here and now, but we want to relate to trends in another way. We are constantly looking ahead while always trying to keep our feet solidly on the ground. A consistent style inspired by contemporary influences is something that endures over time, and that's how we want to work. Obviously it is a constant balancing act when it comes to creating products that are up to date and timeless at the same time. A product that can handle that type of combination has the potential to become a classic, and then we have somehow succeeded."

Have you and your husband Thomas Asplund applied this more thoughtful mindset when it comes to your own home?

"It's kind of funny because we bought our house rather spontaneously. We were invited to friends on Lidingö [a suburban island just outside central Stockholm]. There were some house showings there the same day, and that's when we saw our house for the first time. It was a Thursday, and by Tuesday we had bought it. The house is a simple 1950s split-level villa and we thought it was perfect in all its simplicity. However, the interior was worn and shabby, so we had to tear out and redo the entire upstairs right away. Over the years, we have made a number of changes because our needs change all the time – for example, as our children grow. The latest project we completed, in the summer of 2017, was building an extension onto the bottom floor."

What were your thoughts about the extension?

"I am very interested in architecture, and we have continually thought about tying the extension into the character of the house.

PHOTOGRAPHY: ANDY LIFFNER STYLING: THOMAS LINGSELL

The room often referred to by the family as »the reading room« contains the Basket armchair by the Bouroullec brothers for Cappellini, and the Zoo side table by Claesson Koivisto Rune for Asplund. The Gatto lamp by Achille Castiglioni for Flos/Asplund sits on top. To the right: The bathroom, which combines marble and cement, houses a basket from Muubs and a stool from Gandia Blasco.

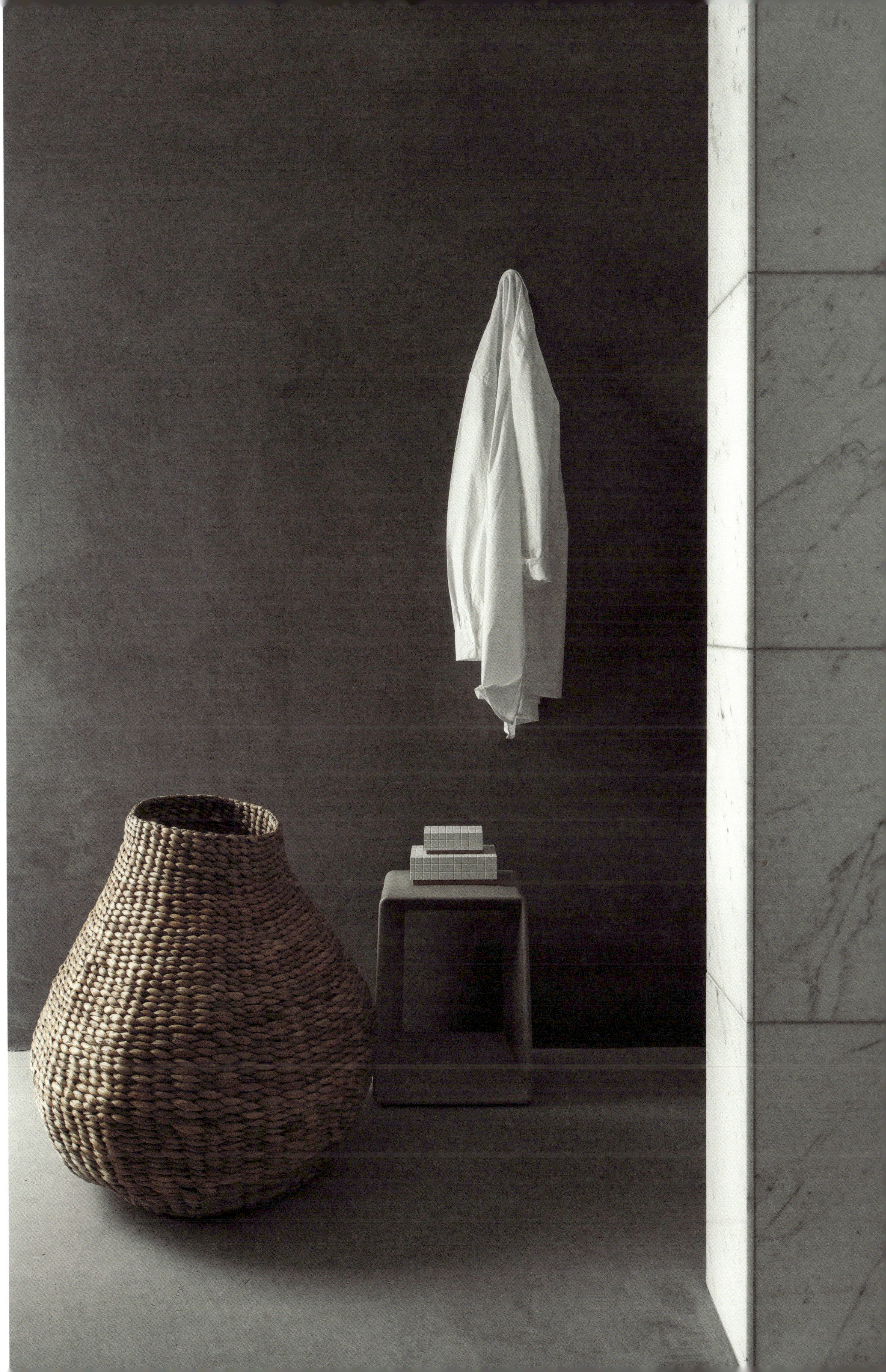

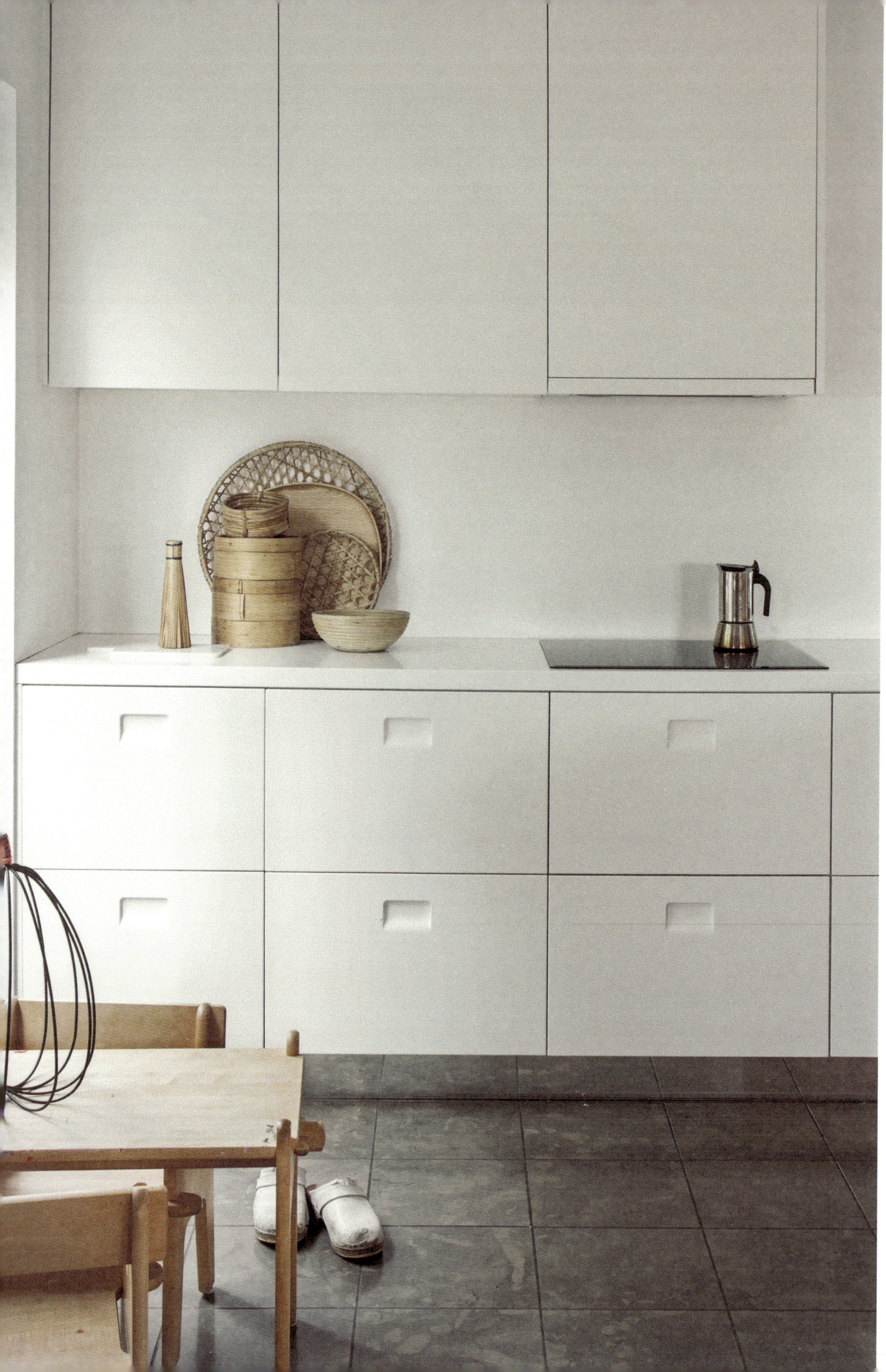

On the terrace is the iconic Thinking Man's Chair designed by Jasper Morrison for Cappellini. The island in the kitchen is constructed in white oil waxed oak, the same material visible on the wall behind Sandra Adrian Asplund. To the left: Asplund's Land kitchen by Johannes Norlander. Table and chairs by Wegner.

Because the new part is an extension of the existing downstairs, which had a concrete floor, we chose to have concrete flooring in the extension as well, and I just love it. Because our style, and perhaps even more my own, is so minimalist, materials are extremely important. Concrete with wood creates a contrast that gives life and depth, heat and coolness."

What is important to you at home?

"That despite the minimalist style, there is a personality that shines through. I like to add things with history and unusual details. I probably have a background story for every gadget and piece of furniture at home. In addition to that, for me it's a lot about creating the right atmosphere."

How do you create it?

"By using light and proper flow. There always needs to be balance. It may sound abstract, but I can feel instantly when something does not work. We have three long corridors in the house that contribute to the flow. Windows at each end of the hallways let in light, and doors that open towards the outer walls are sliding doors; we have no ordinary doors or thresholds. Now that we've built the downstairs, everything feels just as good as I'd imagined it would. There is a peaceful feeling all over the house, and even though it's built for socialising, there's always a place to retreat if you want to be alone. It's hard to put your finger on what really creates this peaceful feeling, but if you're standing in one place you can somehow get a feeling for the entire house without knowing every nook and cranny."

By Rebecca Öhnfeldt

Back in the 1920s, Swedish publisher Erik Åkerlund built a castle-like property in Dalarö, outside Stockholm. Now Swedish company BTH is building residential apartments in the mythical halls. The floor plan in the nine apartments was created by architectural firm Christian Halleröd Design, with interior design by Lotta Agaton.

Villa Åkerlund
RUXANDRA HALLERÖD & LOTTA AGATON

VILLA ÅKERLUND IN Dalarö, in Stockholm's southern archipelago, is the closest you can get to the feel of the Great Gatsby in Sweden. Located at the edge of the cliff overlooking the bay, the extravagant property evokes the sumptuous celebrations depicted in F. Scott Fitzgerald's timeless tale, set in America's Long Island between the two world wars. Here in the old archipelago community – where one of Sweden's foremost artists, Anders Zorn, created a number of paintings, and the great dramatist August Strindberg recuperated after his various crises – wealthy publisher and entrepreneur Erik Åkerlund built his castle-like villa in the 1920s. Rising over Dalarö's small cottages and summer residences, the house was woven into legends about the festivities of the beautiful people, about a life of luxury and a sunken piano. Erik Åkerlund lived a life of high intensity and went out with a bang. During a party in 1940, he blew a hunting horn so hard that he suffered a brain haemorrhage and died a few days later, at the age of 63. His wine cellar apparently contained 280 bottles of champagne.

Many years later, Swedish property developer BTH Bostad saw the opportunity to develop the mythical site. Work is underway to turn the Åkerlund residence into nine exclusive flats. The new floor plan is by Christian Halleröd Design, famous for creating shop furnishings across Sweden and internationally. The interior design is by Sweden's celebrated interior stylist Lotta Agaton.

The Swedish real estate market has experienced a major boom over the past few years, with a growing number of property developers collaborating with well-appointed architects and interior designers to offer comprehensive housing solutions in the emerging premium sector – including exclusive condominiums in former public schools and factories and a series of high level renovations.

Agaton has broad experience in this area. For her, the work at the Åkerlund residence has focused on the soul of the house and transforming the building into luxurious accommodation while preserving the original atmosphere. "We have worked closely with the local architectural curator," says Agaton. "Although the interior is not landmarked, we want to preserve as much of this magnificent environment as possible." The nine flats in the villa are by architect Ruxandra Halleröd, of Christian Halleröd Design, who previously worked in the design department of Swedish real estate company Oscar Properties. "It was great to come here and see the house in real life," says Halleröd. "The concept is to recreate the feeling in the old rooms by trying to keep the external lines intact. When all the doors are open, you can see the original room volumes."

RUXANDRA HALLERÖD & LOTTA AGATON | MY RESIDENCE 147

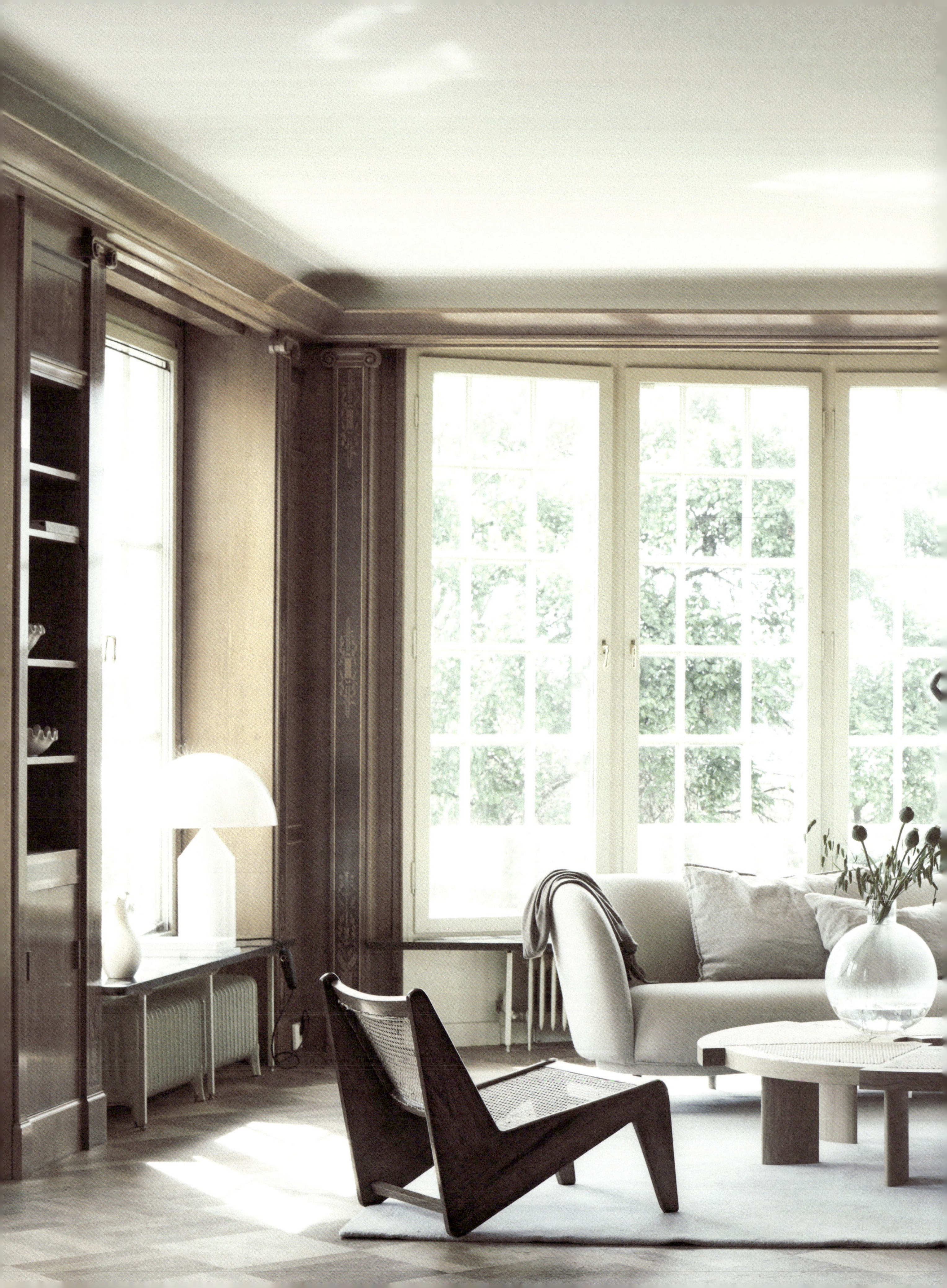

The sculpture in the window reflects the history of the villa. The rattan armchairs are by Pierre Jeanneret, from Galerie Maison Première. The Dandy sofa is from Massproductions, and the Rio coffee table is by Charlotte Perriand, from Nordiska Galleriet.

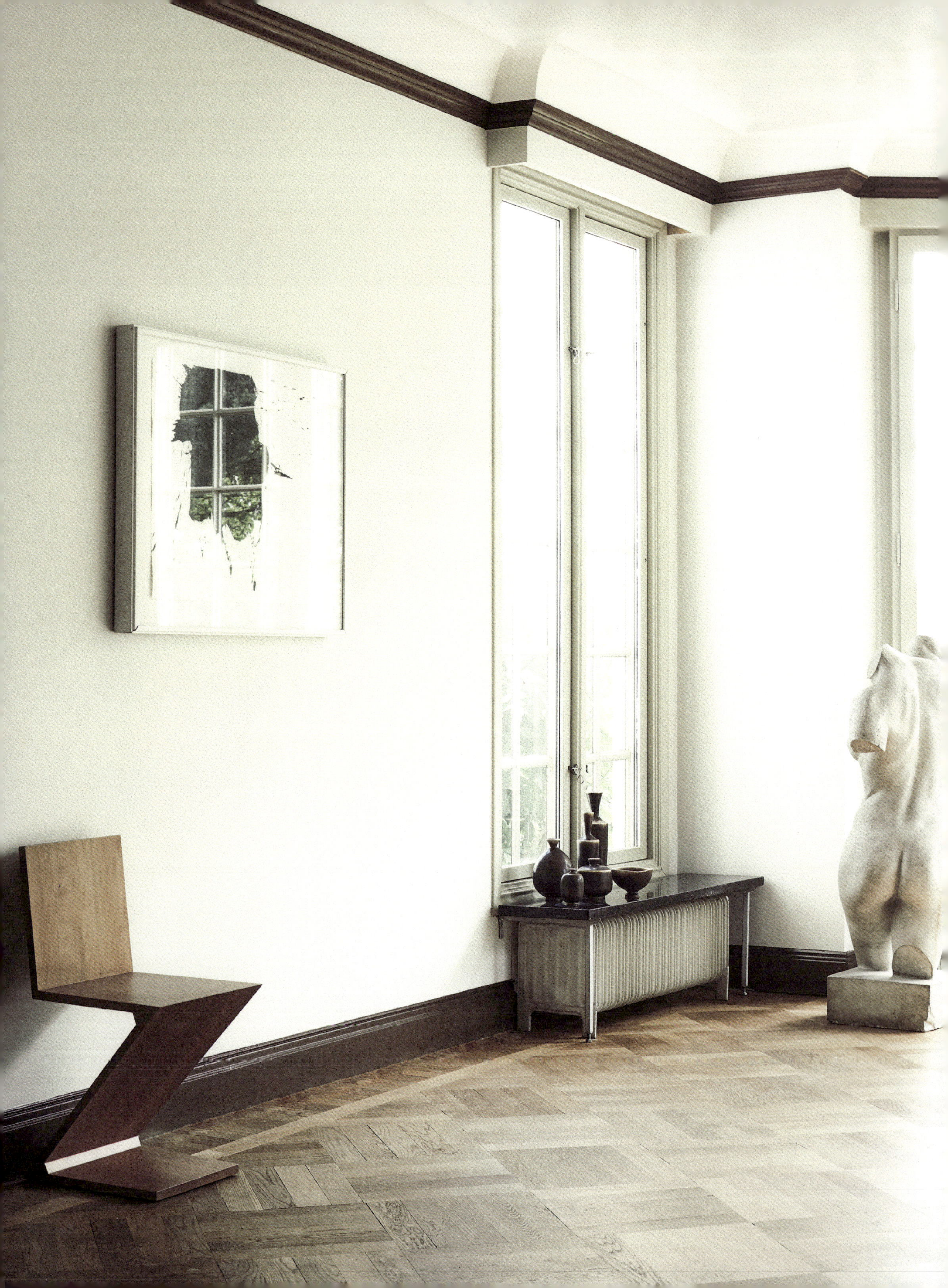

The Atollo lamp from Oluce stands in the window. There is a view out over the Stockholm archipelago and a beautiful flow of natural light in every room. To the left: A sculpture by Anders Jönsson. Against the wall is the Zig-Zag chair by Gerrit T. Rietveld, from Nordiska Galleriet, with a painting by Rune Hagberg, from Modernity.

The villa had already been remodelled several times during the Åkerlund era. Despite being used for school activities for 50 years before it was bought by BTH, a lot of the former luxury survived in the form of ornate oak panels, fireplaces and painted glass windows, with the motifs of Erik Åkerlund's favourite hobbies: sailing, hunting and curling. The flats at Villa Åkerlund will be ready for occupancy in December 2018, with many original details preserved. In the villa's park, BTH's other project, Lyngsåsa, is also taking shape. Here there will be 13 properties containing 51 flats, designed by Swedish firm Brunnberg & Forshed as a modern take on Dalarö archipelago-style architecture. Construction cranes are rising all over Dalarö to deal with its housing shortage, and the area will soon be enriched with an entirely new neighbourhood.

By Petter Eklund

We are happy to introduce two rug collections Duet and Villa La Madonna, enhanced with wool and glitter yarn, creating a softer look and feel.
See our new rug collections at bolon.com

BOLON

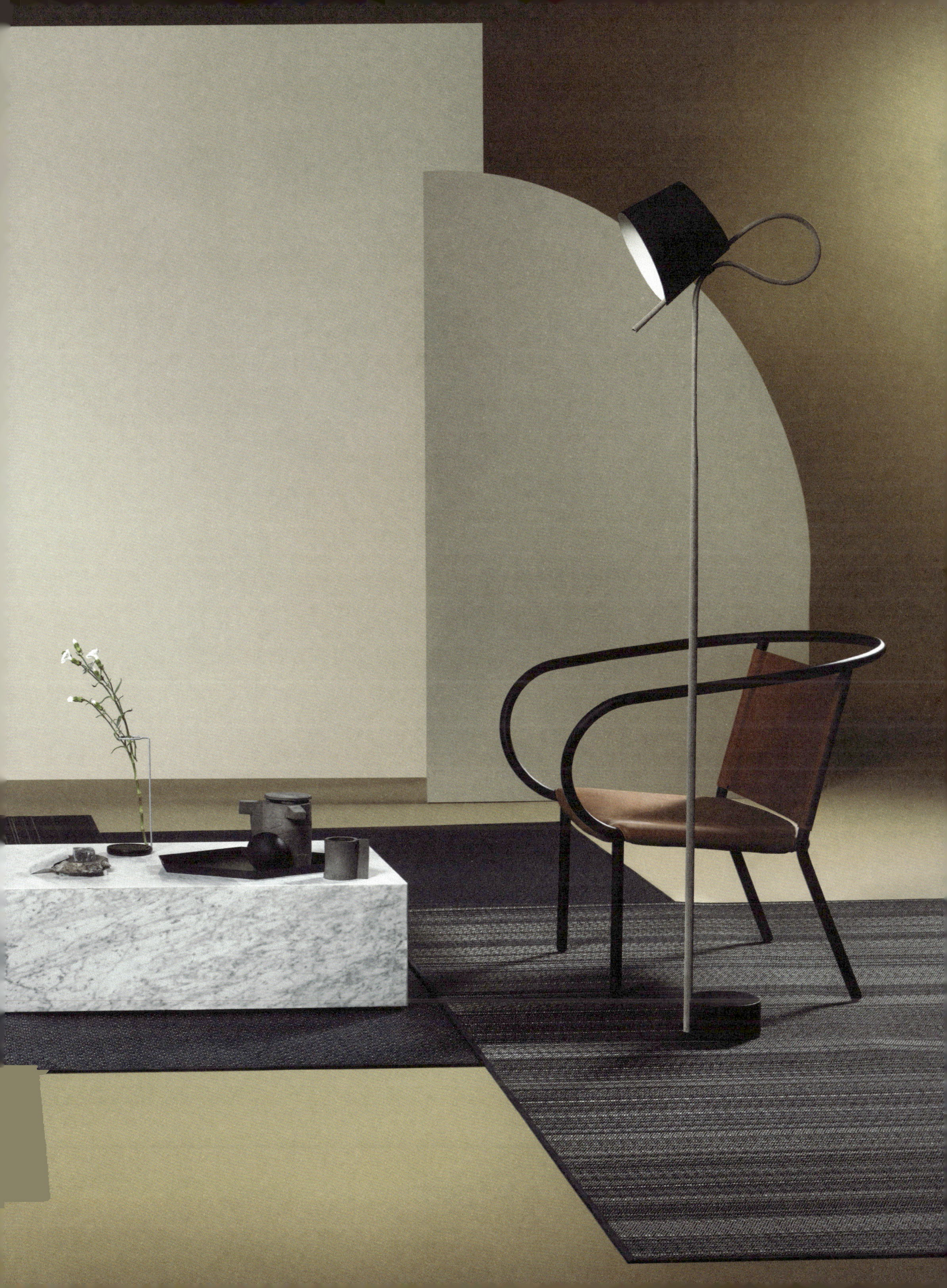

KVÄNUM

BROBY
ASH GREY
SOFT WHITE

WWW.KVANUM.COM

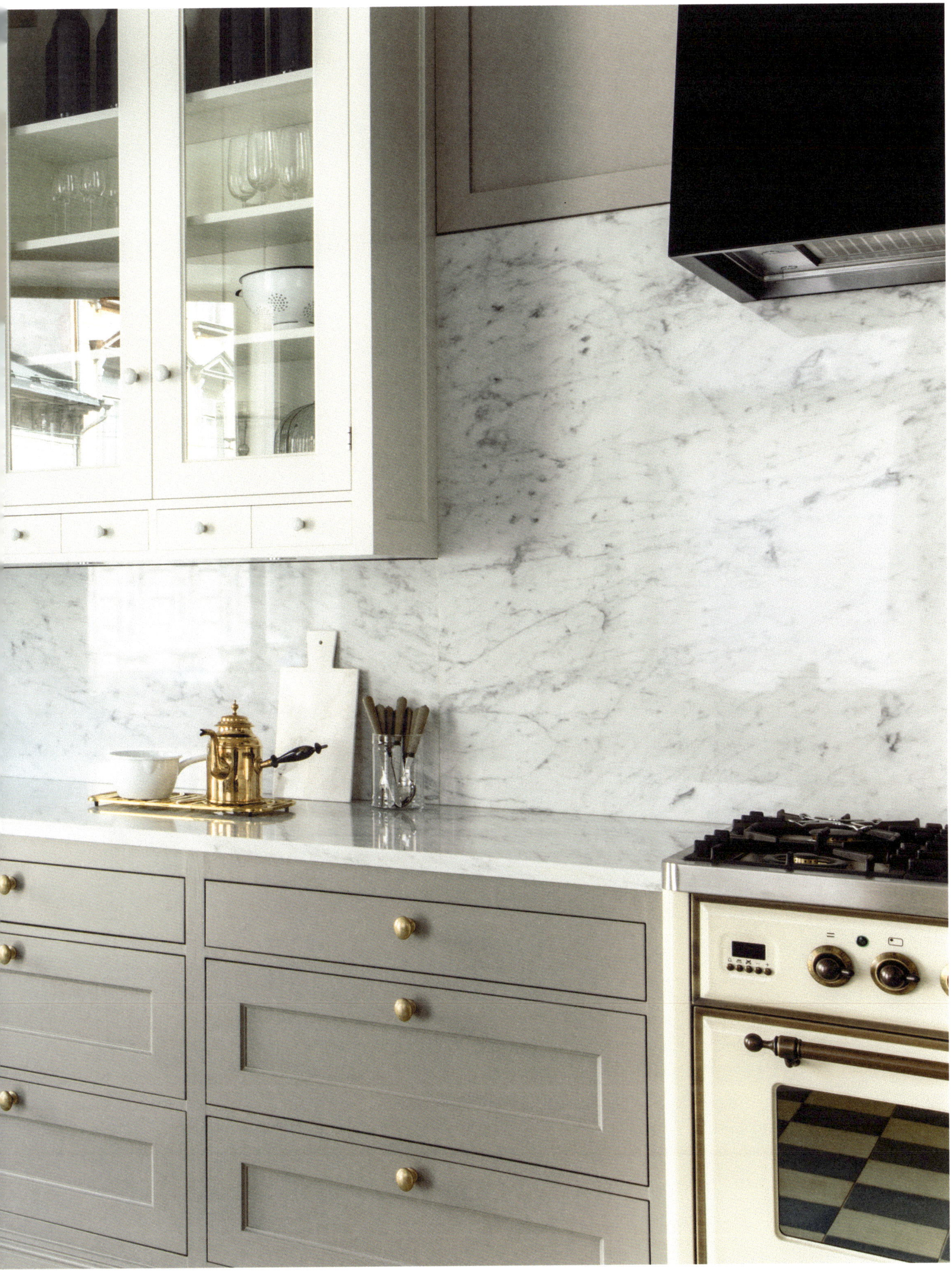

VOLA AB Showroom
Storgatan 24
S-114 55 Stockholm
Tel.: 08- 660 2801
sales@vola.se
www.vola.se

Easily adaptable to any space, the multiple award-winning Round-head shower is the epitome of modern product design. Designed for maximum coverage, whether wall- or ceiling-mounted, the 060 delivers high performance in an elegant, efficient and minimal form, with an array of finish options to suit every design scheme.

vola®

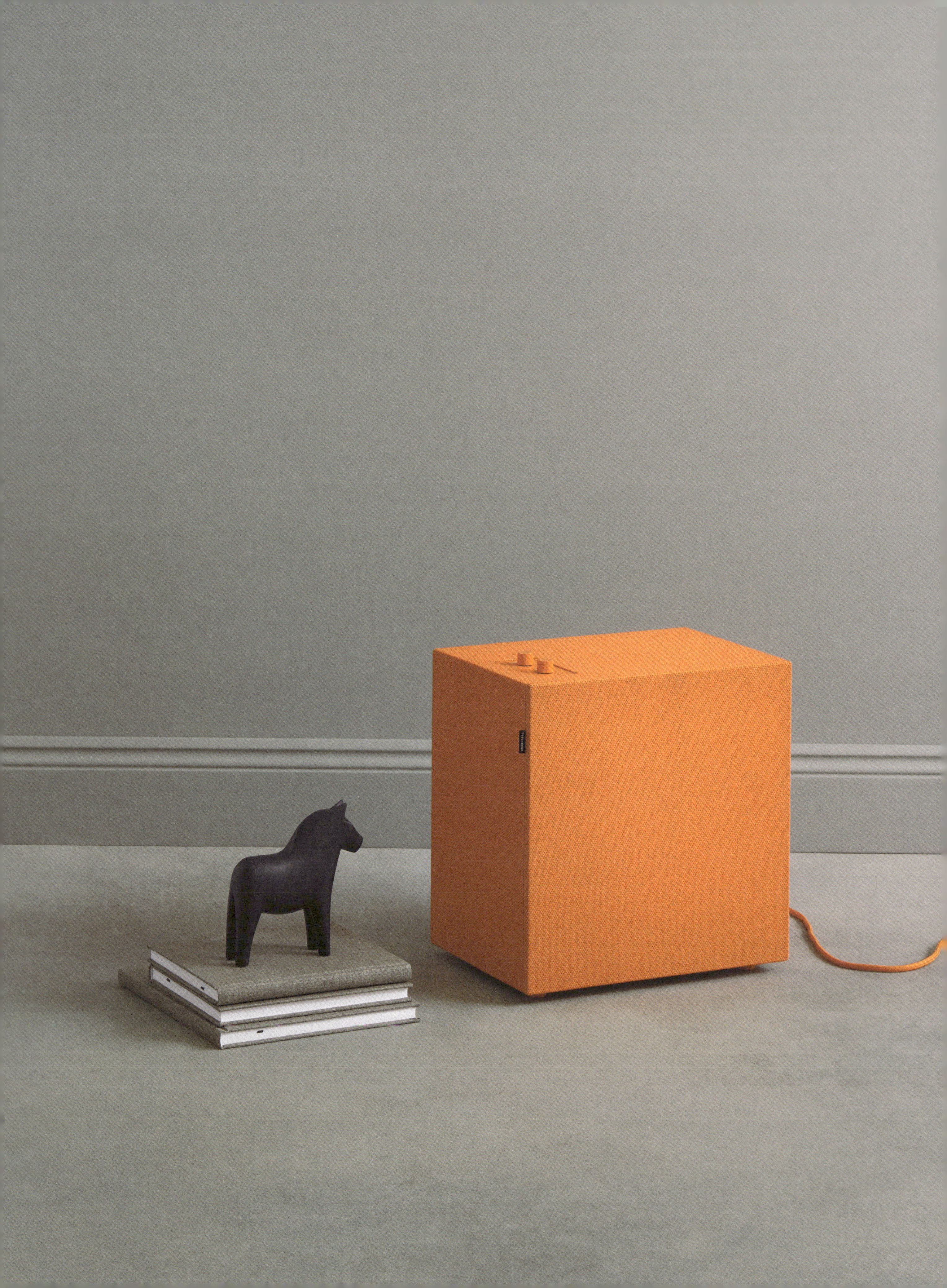

Multiroom speakers that complement your home

URBANEARS
www.urbanears.com

THE ROMO GROUP
Diversity of Style

ROMO
romo.com

ROMO · BLACK edition · kirkby design · Mark Alexander · VILLA NOVA · zinc

WE WILL ALWAYS BE MODERN, OUR DESIGN ALWAYS ESSENTIAL

LAMMHULTS

APERI | DESIGN JULIA LÄUFER & MARCUS KEICHEL, 2016

LAMMHULTS.SE
PART OF LAMMHULTS DESIGN GROUP